A Guide to Writing
Sociology Papers

SEVENTH EDITION

The Sociology Writing Group

COORDINATOR AND EDITOR
William G. Roy

AUTHORS
Roseann Giarrusso
Judith Richlin-Klonsky
William G. Roy
Ellen Strenski

WORTH PUBLISHERS
A Macmillan Higher Education Company

Senior Vice President, Editorial and Production: Catherine Woods
Publisher: Kevin Feyen
Associate Publisher: Jessica Bayne
Acquisitions Editor: Sarah Berger
Developmental Editor: Michelle McIlvoy
Editorial Assistant: Katherine Garrett
Executive Marketing Manager: Katherine Nurre
Marketing Coordinator: Julie Tompkins
Art Director: Babs Reingold
Senior Designer: Kevin Kall
Cover Designer: Lissi Sigillo
Interior Designer: Bobby Starnes, ElectraGraphics, Inc.
Director of Development for Print and Digital Products: Tracey Kuehn
Associate Managing Editor: Lisa Kinne
Project Editor: Robert Errera
Production Manager: Barbara Anne Seixas
Composition: ElectraGraphics, Inc.
Printing and Binding: RR Donnelley

Library of Congress Cataloging-in-Publication Data Control Number: 2013942907
ISBN-13: 978-1-4292-3479-5
ISBN-10: 1-4292-3479-2
© 2013, 2008, 2001, 1998 by Worth Publishers

Worth Publishers
41 Madison Avenue
New York, NY 10010
www.worthpublishers.com

CONTENTS

PART 1 ESSENTIALS

PART 2 WORKING WITH SOURCES

PART 3 WRITING FROM VARIOUS DATA SOURCES

TO THE INSTRUCTOR

*A Guide to Writing Sociology Paper*s has been extremely well received by instructors in a wide range of sociology courses since the publication of the First Edition. Both instructors and countless students have benefited from its clear, straightforward, and engaging style.

The craft of writing is universally embraced as one of the premier skills of a college education. Even in the age of 140-character tweets, social texting, and information overload, writing remains at the heart of critical thinking and deep learning. Surveys of those who hire college graduates consistently identify writing as one of the skills they wish colleges would teach more effectively. When faculty members describe the ideal student, he or she is typically one who writes well. Students, in turn, often describe writing achievement as their greatest source of pride and their most enduring learning experience. Yet faculty members sometimes despair of their ability to teach writing. Even when they have earnestly worked at their own writing skills, many feel poorly equipped to cultivate their students' talents. And many who have taught writing to students realize that they cannot do it alone.

FLEXIBLE DESIGN

A Guide to Writing Sociology Papers grew out of our collective experiences as sociology and English faculty members, teaching assistants, counselors, and tutors at UCLA. The book is designed to relieve you of some of the burden of writing instruction and to provide your students—from beginning to advanced—with practical advice. Its format is flexible enough to accommodate specific modifications, yet "spelled out" enough to guide those who need to pay special attention to all steps in the writing process, from initial conceptualization to final presentation.

WRITING AS EXERCISING THE SOCIOLOGICAL IMAGINATION

The underlying premise of the book is that thinking and writing are integrally related and, therefore, that writing a sociology paper involves exercising the "sociological imagination." Throughout the book, our advice and examples are informed by this practical pedagogical observation. When instructors comment to students that their papers "are too psychological" or "really don't address a sociological issue," for example, students tend to be confused and rarely learn how to correct the problem in later papers. Similarly, comments that a paper "has no structure," "follows no clear logic," or "lacks sufficient evidence" often baffle students. Our goal here is to provide both you and your students with illustrations and a common language for discussing and improving papers in these areas.

ACCESSIBILITY TO STUDENTS

This book can be used in a variety of ways in both lower- and upper-division sociology courses. For example, you can assign it as a resource for students to consult on their own. Or you can refer in class or in discussion sections to specific parts, explaining how students can apply our advice to your assignment and how our sample student papers do or do not represent what you expect. Or, in your comments on drafts or in individual conferences with students, you can direct students to specific pages in the text.

In addition, the book can be used in a range of writing classes from developmental to advanced. It is especially appropriate for adjunct writing courses paired with sociology courses. However, since much of the advice we present can be generalized to other disciplines, the book is also suitable as a basic text in advanced writing courses that emphasize the social sciences. Much of the book—Chapters 2, 3, 4, 5, and 6 and Part 4—applies equally to courses in the humanities.

STUDENT-FRIENDLY WRITING STYLE

Although we focus on the priorities most commonly identified by instructors, our own writing style is intentionally "student friendly." Students report that learning about writing is sometimes boring or intimidating. Thus, our tone is deliberately easygoing, avoiding prohibitions where possible, and offering guidelines rather than commandments. We also include many concrete examples, some taken from student papers, to make the guidelines less abstract.

A NOTE ABOUT THE SEVENTH EDITION

The biggest change in this edition is a thorough revision oriented toward the technology-savvy student. Previous editions continued to reflect the book's origins in a time when students were finding all their material in the library and taking notes on 3×5 cards. This edition encourages students to visit their libraries, but assumes that most students will do so only after exhausting online sources. Most will draft, edit, and refine papers on their computers. They are probably more comfortable exchanging e-mails with faculty members than visiting them in their offices. While embracing the information revolution, we realize the importance of cultivating critical assessment of online outlets in both finding sources and using them.

On that note we have developed a new Part 2, "Working with Sources." Chapter 4, "Collecting and Evaluating Sources," includes expanded coverage on finding sources on the Web, with an explicit discussion of Wikipedia. Some students don't fully understand the underlying principles of plagiarism or the fine distinctions between acceptable and unacceptable use of other people's words. In Chapter 5, "Citing Sources and Preparing Bibliographies," we have expanded our discussion about why it is important to credit others for their ideas and clarified the appropriate ways to borrow, keeping in mind the new challenges of using material from the Web.

Some chapter sections have moved following helpful suggestions by reviewers. In Part 1, "The Essentials," we have added a new Chapter 2, "Designing Your Paper," which addresses issues relevant to the overall structure of the paper, including logic, introductions and conclusions, overall format, analytical terms often used in assignments, and how to write a paper proposal. Chapter 1, "Getting Started," now focuses on understanding and exercising the sociological imagination and framing a good paper question. Chapter 3, "The Writing Process," has a fuller discussion of how to sculpt ideas into writing and a new discussion of academic writing styles. Chapter 9, titled "The Ethnographic Field Research Paper" in the Sixth Edition, has been thoroughly revised and is now called "The Qualitative Research Paper." It still focuses on ethnographic research but also addresses issues of qualitative writing beyond ethnography.

Finally, we have changed the design of the sample student papers so that author comments are now boxed in the margin, making the reading process easier. We have also added helpful notes and encouraging or insightful quotations throughout in the margins of the text.

ACKNOWLEDGMENTS

Special thanks go to the students who granted us permission to use all or part of their work as examples: Lysa Agundez, Tanaya Burnham, Mayank Chawla, Christina De Roulhac, Gloria Fong, Dana E. Knickerbocker, and Shannon Prior.

Profound thanks are also due to Arlene Dallalfar, Lisa Frohmann, and Nancy A. Matthews, contributors to previous editions of *A Guide to Writing Sociology Papers*. We continue to be inspired by the commitment to teaching of our friend and colleague Constance Coiner (1948–1996), who contributed in a major way to the First Edition of this book.

Lee Ann Carroll, Professor Emerita of English at Pepperdine University, made a major contribution to the discussion of the writing process, not only commenting on the last edition but also contributing ideas and language that were incorporated into the text. Alice M. Roy, Professor Emerita of English at California State University, Los Angeles, read several drafts of each chapter and expertly suggested numerous improvements to the text.

We would like to acknowledge our gratitude to the following professors who assisted in the revision of this book by responding to our questions about the previous edition: Robert Bulman, Saint Mary's College; Charles Cappell, Northern Illinois University; Jeffrey Chin, Le Moyne College; Vicky L. Elias, Texas A&M University, San Antonio; Elizabeth Anne Jenner, Gustavus Adolphus College; Karen Kendrick, Albertus Magnus College; Patricie E. Literte, California State University, Fullerton; Ethel G. Nicdao, University of the Pacific; Michelle Owen, University of Winnipeg; and Karen Van Gundy, University of New Hampshire.

Many of the enhancements in this edition can be credited to the staff at Worth Publishers. Sarah Berger has energetically and insightfully nurtured the revision, gently prodding when needed, suggesting improvements, encouraging the authors at just the right time, and attending to details that authors try their hardest to avoid. If there was a picture in the dictionary for "editor" it should be Sarah. Michelle McIlvoy patiently and skillfully refined the prose, finding and eliminating redundancy, excess verbiage, and infelicity. The book is more readable for her efforts.

ABOUT THE AUTHORS

The members of the Sociology Writing Group came together in 1984 to prepare a guide for instructors and students in sociology and writing courses at UCLA. *A Guide to Writing Sociology Papers* grew out of this collaborative effort.

Roseann Giarrusso is Associate Professor of Sociology at California State University, Los Angeles, where she teaches courses in social gerontology, research methods, writing for sociology, and social psychology. She is also a consultant at the Andrus Gerontology Center at the University of Southern California, where she conducts longitudinal research on intergenerational family relationships. Most of her more than 50 publications apply a social psychological perspective to the study of family relationships and aging.

Judith Richlin-Klonsky has taught sociology for more than 25 years at institutions including UCLA, UCSD, Sonoma State University, and Santa Rosa Junior College. Her favorite courses include the sociology of everyday life, race and ethnic relations, group processes, medical sociology, and the sociology of mental illness. She has published research on psychotherapy professions and on family relationships, as well as conducted institutional research on the experiences and needs of college students. Judith Richlin-Klonsky holds a master's degree in family therapy and received her Ph.D. in sociology from UCLA, specializing in qualitative research methods and an interpretive theoretical framework.

William G. Roy is Professor Emeritus of Sociology at UCLA, winner of the 1989 UCLA Award for Distinguished Teaching, and the American Sociological Association Distinguished Contribution to Teaching Award. He is author of *Socializing Capital: The Rise of the Large Industrial Corporation in America* (Princeton University Press, 1997), *Making Societies: The Historical Construction of Our World* (Pine Forge Press, 2001) and *Reds, Whites, and Blues: Social Movements, Folk Movements, and Race in the United States* (Princeton University Press, 2010). His specialties include the sociology of music and comparative-historical sociology, particularly long-term political and economic transformations. He oversaw the revision of the Seventh Edition.

Ellen Strenski has been Composition Director in the English Department at the University of California at Irvine. In addition to coauthoring *The Research Paper Workbook* (New York: Longman, 3rd ed., 1991) and *Making Connections across the Curriculum: Readings for Analysis* (Boston: Bedford, 1986), she has published articles in many pedagogical journals on the subject of writing in diverse disciplines. Most recently, she has exercised her sociological imagination in several articles and chapters that analyze issues in writing-program administration.

TO THE STUDENT

If you're uneasy about the prospect of writing a sociology paper, you're not alone. Many students feel as you do; that's why we wrote this book. We can't promise that your assignment will be easy, but it can be done, and done well. This book can help you feel in control of the writing process from beginning to end, and it can help you produce your best work. Even if daunting at first, writing a sociology paper can be highly rewarding, producing both the pleasure of learning and the gratification of achievement. Developing writing skill is one of the fundamental feats of college education—a skill needed in nearly all professional careers.

We've written the guide we wish we'd had as undergraduates. We experienced many problems in writing our own papers, and we want to spare you some of the trouble we endured. And we have learned that procrastination—our own and that of others—is not always the result of laziness but is often a sign of uncertainty about just how to begin and complete a writing task. Our personal experience as writers and teachers has also shown that writing can be improved with effort. Although some people may appear to be "natural-born writers," everyone can become a better writer by self-consciously working at it. This book does not prescribe any one correct process of writing but recognizes that different students work in different ways. Regardless of whether you write a "spew draft" and then revise, make an outline to fill in, or use any other method, this book is intended to help you in each of the skills that contribute to the best work you can do.

WHAT YOUR INSTRUCTOR EXPECTS

Our students often tell us that they don't know what they're expected to do in a paper or that they don't know what the instructor wants. So we've tried to demystify the process. We encapsulate what makes a paper sociological and how sociology differs from other disciplines. We suggest ways to get started and to stay on track, ways to deal with and present your data, ways to troubleshoot your writing, and ways to make your prose look and sound professional. All along the way our book gives practical illustrations, including sample student papers that you can compare with your own. These sample papers are very good, but they are not perfect. We comment on their fine features and suggest alternatives where problems remain.

We recommend that everyone read all the chapters in Part 1, "Essentials," and Part 4, "Finishing Up," and refer to the chapters in Part 2, "Working with Sources," as needed. The chapters in Part 3, "Writing from Various Data Sources," can be used selectively. Use the table of contents and the index to find what you're looking for.

GETTING STARTED

Part 1, "Essentials," includes chapters on the essential aspects of writing. Chapter 1 focuses on the conceptual starting points that are fundamental for writing a good sociology paper—understanding the sociological imagination and asking a good question. Chapter 2 focuses on the big picture of paper writing, including the importance of logic and structure, understanding key terms on exam or essay assignments, and writing a proposal for a paper. Chapter 3 instructs you in developing a process for writing, conquering writer's block, and revising. The two chapters in Part 2, "Working with Sources," advise you on collecting, evaluating, and citing sources in your paper and preparing bibliographies. These chapters also present guidelines for keeping track of notes and references to avoid plagiarism. Follow these guidelines from the beginning of your project.

DOING YOUR RESEARCH AND WRITING IT UP

Part 3 includes chapters on the four typical kinds of sociology papers that are, in turn, based on four different types of sources: textual analysis (Chapter 6), general research (Chapter 7), quantitative research (Chapter 8), and qualitative research (Chapter 9). All four chapters contain student papers as illustrations.

FINISHING UP

Part 4, "Finishing Up," includes guidelines on editing and formatting your paper, a checklist for your final draft, and suggestions for expanding your sociological imagination.

HOW TO USE THIS BOOK

Don't try to read the whole book at one go. The four chapters in Part 3 are meant to guide you through steps in a process. Use these chapters as you would instructions for assembling anything: first scan the chapter to get a sense of what you're in for and then consult it carefully as you move along step by step. Sometimes a writing assignment can loom as an enormous, mysterious undertaking because students don't know how to break it down into smaller, more manageable tasks. This guide does that for you. There may be portions of the guide that you'll have to reread before they make sense to you and other portions that you'll refer to again and again for present and future writing assignments.

The primary purpose of this book is to help you prepare good sociology papers, and, except for Chapter 8 on quantitative research, which is more technical than the other chapters, you'll be able to use this book from day one of any sociology course. But you'll also find that much of this book applies as well to other social sciences and that many parts of it will even help you write papers in the humanities. *A Guide to Writing Sociology Papers* will help you from the start to the finish of your college career.

OTHER SUGGESTIONS

Your own campus may offer other resources to help you further.

+ Find out if your library offers tutorials on information literacy or how to use information sources. Many colleges and universities have in-person and online resources to help students find materials in the library and online, including specialized electronic databases such as *Sociological Abstracts*. Also find out if the library offers a proxy server that allows you remote access to these and other resources. The most useful portals to academic sources are typically available only from a university computer or with a proxy server. A short time invested at the beginning of the quarter or semester when schedules tend to be less demanding may save you many hours later.

✦ Find out if your English department or writing program offers composition courses. Investigate writing courses even if you have fulfilled the requirement for English composition. At some colleges, special writing courses are attached to sociology and other courses, a combination that benefits you doubly. If you are concerned that your present writing skills might earn a less-than-satisfactory grade in a composition class, check out the possibility of taking the course as an elective on a pass/no-pass basis.

✦ Find out if your campus has a tutoring center at which peer or professional tutors can review your work with you and help you strengthen your writing skills.

A NOTE ON OUR WRITING STYLE

Before going on, we would like you to note two features of our writing style: our occasional use of contractions (for example, "we've" instead of "we have") and our avoidance of sexist language.

First, we have tried to make this book as down to earth and practical as possible. We imagine ourselves talking to you as we talk to our own students—trying to be direct, friendly, and helpful. Our prose is therefore informal and includes contractions. Academic papers, on the other hand, have a different purpose and are usually more formal. Some instructors might object to your using contractions in a formal sociology paper.

Second, we have deliberately used inclusive language when we refer to people in general. Historically, masculine nouns and pronouns have been used to refer to women and men both—for example, "Man is a social animal." As a result of the women's movement, this usage has become unacceptable.

Finally, we wish we could show you some of the drafts of this book. Writing anything worthwhile—a paper or a book—is always a frustrating, creative, and rewarding process. Our own experience has been typical. Final written work usually looks so straightforward that it's easy to forget all the drafts and revisions. So don't be discouraged if you don't like what you first write. That's normal. The paper will improve, and you will like it better with each succeeding draft. *A Guide to Writing Sociology Papers* will show you how this happens as it guides you through the writing process.

ESSENTIALS

Perhaps the most disabling myth about intellectual activity is that writing is an art that is prompted by inspiration. Some writing can be classified as an art, no doubt, but the art of writing is a trade in the same sense that plumbing and automotive repair are trades. Just as plumbers and mechanics would rarely accomplish anything if they waited for inspiration to impel them to action, so writers would rarely write if they relied on inspiration.

RODNEY STARK
Sociology

Writing is a craft as well as an art. As with any other craft, becoming a good writer requires understanding the principles of how papers work. A first-rate plumber must know some principles of hydraulics, and an outstanding auto mechanic, the principles of combustion. Writing a good sociology paper requires understanding principles of both sociology and writing.

Part 1 presents these fundamentals of craftsmanship. Chapter 1, "Getting Started," explains topics that might be considered as much inspiration as perspiration, such as how to use a "sociological imagination" in writing and how to frame your paper so that it addresses a sociological question.

Chapter 2, "Designing Your Paper," steps back from writing to discuss paper design. Just as you should not try to build a house without a blueprint, you should not write a paper without a design. Specifically, this chapter covers writing qualities like logic and structure that instructors are looking for but students have difficulty grasping and presenting when writing their papers.

Chapter 3, "The Writing Process," gets to the basics of writing. It offers strategies for getting started—how to organize your time, what to do sitting in front of a blank screen, how to create an outline, how to build a paragraph, and how to write a draft. It also reviews academic style. These chapters should be useful for all academic writing, not just sociological papers, though they are written from a sociology perspective.

CHAPTER ONE

Getting Started

Additionally, and especially in the social sciences, much unclear writing is based on unclear or incomplete thought. It is possible with safety to be technically obscure about something you haven't thought out. It is impossible to be wholly clear on something you do not understand.

JOHN KENNETH GALBRAITH
Writing, Typing, and Economics

Writing a good sociology paper starts with asking a good sociological question. Choosing a topic is just the beginning of planning your paper. You need to frame your paper's topic in the form of a *question.* The clearer and more explicit the questions are, the clearer and more complete your thinking and writing will be to the reader.

Asking a good question will make the other tasks of writing your paper easier and will help you hand in a well-written product. Think of taking a photograph. The deepest artistic sensitivity or the most sophisticated technical skills cannot create a beautiful picture unless you point the camera in the right direction. But carefully aiming the camera in the right direction combined with simple competence and a personal point of view can produce a breathtaking photograph. Likewise, when you create

a sociology paper, you can produce interesting, high-quality results: the key is to take the time to "point" your work in an effective direction by asking a well-formulated question.

Three features distinguish a question that will serve as a strong foundation for a sociology paper. First, a well-formulated question reflects an understanding of sociology's distinctive perspective on human life. Second, it is carefully posed and framed. Third, it is asked in a way that lends itself to a logical and well-structured answer. This is in contrast to a question that suggests an endless list, such as "What are all the roles adopted by leaders?" or one that is too open-ended, such as "Why are people irrational?" This chapter will help you to meet the first two of these three criteria for asking good questions. The following chapter will address the third criterion.

WHAT IS SOCIOLOGY?

A failure to understand what sociology is and what sociologists do is one reason that students experience difficulty in writing successful sociology papers.
Even though higher education is becoming more interdisciplinary, individual
disciplines such as sociology provide coherent ways of thinking that need to
be mastered. Since asking a good sociological question depends on understanding what sociology is, this section defines sociology and discusses how
it differs from other fields.

Sociology is the study of **people doing things together**. This simple description is a strong intellectual frame that guides how we think about social
reality. First, sociology is the *study of people*. A statement like "new technologies have revolutionized the way people find mates" is not fully sociological
because it is about what things do. A sociological perspective would assume
that what changes the way people mate is how people use the technologies,
not the technologies themselves. Sociology is not just about the human condition, or human instinct, or existence, or even what is inside people's heads,
but about what they *do* (including how they talk). Often people will act differently from what they say they believe. Sociologists want to understand
why. The most challenging part of the definition is the word, "together."
Sociology is about *relations*, the interaction *between* people or groups or societies. Race, for example, is not just about being African American, Asian
American, Native American, or white. It is about people interacting with one
another through their racial identities. As you write and research your papers remember the definition of sociology as "people doing things together."

THE SOCIOLOGICAL IMAGINATION

Another way to describe what is distinctive about a sociological point of view
is the "sociological imagination," a phrase coined by C. Wright Mills ([1959]
2000). Using the sociological imagination means recognizing the connection
between individual, private experience, and the wider society. Mills calls the
personal level an individual's "biography"; he uses the term "history" to refer
to patterns and relationships on the larger scale of society.

As a student, for example, you have followed your own life path to college. Being a college student is part of your personal life story. Your family
has its own beliefs about what a college education means. You have your
own academic and career goals. You have individual feelings and attitudes
about the subjects covered in your classes and your own mixture of college
and work schedules. All these things make up your personal, *biographical*
experience.

Applying sociological imagination to your college life expands your perspective. Using sociological imagination, you can begin to see how your experience as a college student fits into the social world. Perhaps you are part of
a trend in your peer group to major in computer science or communication
studies. It could be that you are part of an ethnic group whose members are

*"The fascination of
sociology lies in the
fact that its perspective
makes us see in a
new light the very
world in which we
have lived all our lives.
This also constitutes
a transformation of
consciousness."*

Peter L. Berger

*Invitation to Sociology:
A Humanistic Perspective*

underrepresented in higher education. Perhaps your academic goals have been affected by social values such as an increasing emphasis on the need for a college degree. Maybe your career choice, combined with many others', will affect the way society's workforce is balanced between producing goods and providing services.

To use sociological imagination is to identify the intersection of biography and history; the ways in which people are affected by social forces, and the ways social groups are affected by their members. According to Mills ([1959] 2000):

> Every individual lives, from one generation to the next, in some society; . . . he [or she] lives out a biography, and . . . he lives it out with some historical sequence. By the fact of his living he contributes, however minutely, to the shaping of his society and its history; even as he is made by society and by its historical push and shove. (P. 6)

Mills's insight—that people both affect their own destiny *and* are swept by currents of history—challenges and eludes sociologists from first-year college students just beginning to study the field to seasoned scholars. The key to using sociological imagination is to stay focused on this relationship.

SOCIOLOGY AND OTHER PERSPECTIVES ON HUMAN BEHAVIOR

Sometimes new students and experienced ones are confused about how sociology is distinguished from other disciplines that study people, such as psychology, political science, history, philosophy, anthropology, and economics. These fields are not totally different. However, we want to focus on what is distinctive about sociology. To write successfully in any discipline, you need to have some idea of its boundaries. Table 1–1 compares and contrasts sociology with psychology, political science, history, philosophy, anthropology, and economics. We have illustrated their differences by showing how researchers in each field might approach one aspect of human life—deviant behavior. Deviant behavior refers to actions and behaviors that violate commonly held values or norms. Most commonly, deviance refers to negative conduct such as crime, drugs, sexual abuse, or mental illness, but some laudatory behavior can be considered deviant if it breaks other norms. For example, priests who follow a vow of poverty, unusually intelligent people, or people who require extreme cleanliness might be considered deviant.

Table 1–1 simplifies the definitions of sociology and its "neighbors," and exaggerates their differences. These differences are intended to sensitize you to sociology's distinctive features; they are not rigidly observed by theorists or researchers.

TABLE 1–1

SOCIOLOGY AND PSYCHOLOGY

Similarities: Both are concerned with attitudes, beliefs, behavior, emotions, and interpersonal relationships.

Differences: Psychology is more likely to focus on the individual level of human behavior, especially the role of biological factors. When sociology considers the individual, it is within the context of social groups.

Studying deviance: Psychologists investigate psychological dispositions that make some people more likely to commit crimes. A sociologist might try to discover whether activities of one socioeconomic class are more likely to be labeled "criminal" than activities of other classes.

SOCIOLOGY AND POLITICAL SCIENCE

Similarities: Both study government.

Differences: Political scientists analyze different forms of government and their underlying philosophies and study the political process. A sociologist is more likely to examine the relationship of the political system to behavior and other aspects of society, such as the economy, religious institutions, and the attitudes of various social groups.

Studying deviance: A political scientist might analyze why groups make choices to support one criminal law over another. A sociologist might examine how such laws change as the members of society adopt different ideological beliefs or how these laws serve the interests of some classes more than others.

SOCIOLOGY AND HISTORY

Similarities: Both look at human life over time.

Differences: Historians are more likely to focus on the influence that individuals have on specific events. Sociologists concentrate on the causes and effects of changes in large-scale patterns of social life, especially institutions such as politics, economy, religion, and education.

Studying deviance: A historian might interpret the motivations and actions of influential deviant individuals and attempt to explain their influence. A sociologist is more likely to trace changes in society's ways of defining and controlling deviant behavior.

SOCIOLOGY AND PHILOSOPHY

Similarities: Both are interested in beliefs about the nature of life.

Differences: Philosophy is a system of abstract reasoning that follows specific rules of logic. Sociology is empirical: it seeks to discover information about the real world by gathering data about what people actually do.

Studying deviance: Philosophers might ask "What is good?" and "What is evil?" or analyze the appropriate uses of the term "deviance." Sociologists focus on what actually goes on in the social world, asking, for instance, "What do members of this particular society or subculture believe is 'right' and 'wrong'?"

SOCIOLOGY AND ANTHROPOLOGY

Similarities: Both are concerned with social life, including culture, beliefs, decision making, relationships, etc.

Differences: Anthropology is more likely to study societies other than our own, and to compare aspects of society cross-culturally.

Studying deviance: Anthropologists might travel to an isolated, nonindustrialized society to study how it defines and treats deviant behavior. Sociologists would study the same processes by focusing on complex, industrial societies.

SOCIOLOGY AND ECONOMICS

Similarities: Both are concerned with how society produces and distributes goods and services.

Differences: An economist concentrates on the economy in its own right, treating it as the aggregation of individual choices. Sociologists are more likely to consider how the economy affects and is affected by other social processes that shape individual choices.

Studying deviance: An economist might study the contributions and costs of deviance to the gross national product. A sociologist might study how the control of the economy by upper social classes provokes deviant behavior, such as burglary and theft, by those without access to a fair share of goods and services.

SOCIOLOGY'S VARYING PERSPECTIVES

One of the major differences between high school and college is that in high school, "learning" means learning facts. Those high school students who demonstrate that they have learned the most facts generally earn the highest grades. In college, however, there is greater emphasis on analytical reasoning and thinking. Students are expected to understand entire systems of knowledge. Moreover, college students find there is more than one way to approach a perspective on a topic.

Intellectual perspectives can differ as well. In the previous section we saw how various disciplines take different perspectives on deviance. They all look at the same behavior, but each discipline paints a different description and develops a different explanation of it. Even *within* sociology there are several perspectives. For example, *microsociological perspectives* consider social life in terms of everyday interaction among small groups of people, while *macrosociological perspectives* see things from the point of view of long-term change and societies as a whole. A microsociological perspective on deviance might ask questions about how people without criminal records interact with ex-convicts, perhaps examining actions that create a sense of shame. A macrosociological perspective might ask why some societies have higher rates of incarceration than others. In C. W. Mills's terms, the microsociologist is looking at crime from the perspective of biography, while the macrosociologist is looking from the perspective of history, but they are both asking sociological questions about criminals. To some extent, these perspectives disagree about what we might consider the "facts" of society—whether it is stable or conflicted, or whether it is defined by what occurs on a large scale or in direct interpersonal relations. More often, different perspectives are simply asking different questions.

Some students struggle with the cognitive ambiguity that can arise when different perspectives with very different implications are all considered acceptable. To be able to juggle more than one perspective in your mind at the same time is one of the great intellectual feats of a college education. As a novice sociologist, your task is to understand these different perspectives and to learn how to support whichever point of view *you* take with empirical evidence.

Sociology not only encompasses a range of perspectives, but also allows sociologists to apply them to questions about an innumerable array of topics. Like other disciplines, sociology has several major subdisciplines or variations on a theme. Sociology may examine events that are as momentary as the eye contact between strangers on a bus or as long-term as the industrialization of society. It may deal with social life in terms of its structure, attempting to uncover stable, underlying patterns, or it may look at the fleeting interactional processes through which individuals relate socially.

In sociology classes you might study anything from the sociology of sports to the sociology of religion. You might learn about how those engaged in different occupations perceive their work lives, how a thief commits a crime, or how children learn table manners. You might study birthrates, medical decision making, or the sex lives of teenagers in the 1930s versus the 21st century. And, for each of these subjects, sociologists may differ on the kinds of questions to ask and the methods used to answer them.

SOCIOLOGICAL METHODS

Sociology's methods vary considerably and there is no "right" way to think sociologically or to do sociological research, as long as it is supported with empirical evidence.

"I don't pretend we have all the answers. But the questions are certainly worth thinking about."

Arthur C. Clarke

Methods, whether in sociology or any other discipline, involve conventions and practices for connecting the world to data or evidence (the process of data collection), analyzing the data, drawing conclusions on the basis of that analysis, and reporting the first three steps to others in writing. Sociologists have a variety of approaches to how this is done. Sometimes they collect quantitative data, which is information transformed into numbers and analyzed statistically. Survey data, for example, can be used to code what age people are and the number of times—if any—they have been in prison for a crime. Quantitative sociologists follow well-codified rules for measuring concepts about people or groups. The analysis typically examines the relationship between selected social variables, such as the relationship between age and criminal behavior, and should be guided by a theory that explains the relationship between variables. For instance, a theory of life-course development might be used to understand why younger men may be expected to commit more crimes than older men. After collecting and analyzing data on prisoners, the researchers might generalize about whether a 20-year-old or a 45-year-old is more likely to end up in prison. They then write it up in a standard article format with a theoretical discussion, a literature review, testable hypotheses, a summary of methods, results, and conclusion, as described in Chapter 8.

Quantitative sociologists tend to be especially concerned about whether their methods allow detailed comparison with other studies on the same topic. More qualitative methods do not convert reality into numbers, but rather observe things directly, either in overt observation or in documents such as newspapers, historical sources, or cultural creations. Rather than statistical analysis, they search for patterns in the evidence they have collected, often stored in field notes. From these patterns, qualitative sociologists figure out whether their results fit or challenge previous research on the topic. When they write up their study, they draw conclusions about confirming or revising theory. In studying deviance, for example, they might ask how individuals who break the law come to see themselves as a criminal (if at all). Or they might explore how social interactions produce different ideas about deviance in different subcultures. To accomplish their goals, these sociologists use qualitative methods, conducting research that is quite different from that done in the biological or physical sciences. Examples of these methods include the participant-observation method and open-ended interviewing (discussed in Chapter 9). Rather than trying to generalize, qualitative sociologists want to specify, in detail, how the social world is constructed. They tend to be more concerned about insights into their particular case, with less emphasis on comparing their findings with other studies.

Despite their different approaches, however, all sociologists base their conclusions on a combination of insight and carefully collected and analyzed evidence. An increasing number of studies explicitly employ mixed methods, trying to answer basic questions from several methodological perspectives.

Although some sociology departments specialize in one perspective, topic, or method, most departments include faculty members who represent a range of sociological concerns and styles. Course curricula, including writing assignments, reflect this variety, and students typically have the opportunity to become familiar with several ways of asking and answering sociological questions.

EVIDENCE

Like other natural and social sciences, sociology expects questions to be answered with evidence, not just speculation or opinion. Theoretical and methodological writing, however, can be an exception. Sociologists are fond of highlighting all the misconceptions about society that "everybody knows." For example, "everybody knows" (wrongly) that lower-class people commit more crimes than middle- or upper-class people. Thus we are conscious about what evidence is reliable to answer sociological questions.

It is important to distinguish between evidence and opinion. Although your teachers are interested in your opinion, they want you to distinguish between it and evidence. Opinion is what a person believes, how he or she feels, and may be based on facts, but is personal or subjective. Opinions often take the form of a fact. "Men are more aggressive than women" can either be an opinion or a conclusion, based on evidence. The critical point about evidence is that it is based on an understanding of how a person knows what they know. Evidence should be based on systematic observation using specific methods such as quantitative analysis, ethnography and other qualitative methods, or comparative and historical methods. Students will usually get information through secondary sources, textbooks, or professors. If someone claims that information is true, it must be substantiated. Chapter 4 elaborates on the kind of sources that can be reliably referenced for sociology papers. The main point is that evidence should be the foundation for answering sociological questions.

FRAMING A QUESTION

Writing a good sociology paper requires using your sociological imagination to frame an interesting question that then guides your research effort. Remember, *a sociological perspective involves seeing people doing things together.* We study people, not just one person at a time. We study *people doing things.* We usually study them as members of groups, whether a couple; a family; an organization; a gender, racial, or ethnic group; a nation; or a global system. As you prepare to formulate the question that will define your sociology paper, remember that *adopting the sociological perspective is always the first step* in writing a successful paper. Asking a sociologically imaginative question is one of the tasks students find most challenging and most difficult. Suggestions to help you write your question include:

"A prudent question is one-half of wisdom."

Francis Bacon

Remember the *history* part of the sociological imagination. Avoid overly individualistic or psychological questions, questions that concern only what happens inside a person's head. For example, asking whether criminals are motivated more by aggression than by greed is more interesting psychologically than sociologically. (We are in no way implying that psychological questions are inferior to sociological questions, but our purpose here is to emphasize the sociological aspects of human life.) A sociologically imaginative question might ask what aspects of social life—such as race, class, or gender—influence people to act out their aggression or greed in socially acceptable or unacceptable ways.

Remember the *biography* part of the sociological imagination. Avoid questions that overlook people. For example, asking how much income is lost to crime each year is less sociologically imaginative than asking what types of crime typically victimize wealthy people as compared with poor people.

Ask a question concerning *differences* between individuals, groups, roles, relationships, societies, or time periods. Only rarely do sociologists make claims about all people or all societies. They are more interested in how and why people of societies differ from one another; they more frequently ask questions about variation than about uniformity. For example, they would probably not ask whether people are by nature aggressive, but, rather, why some people are more aggressive than others. Are highly aggressive people socialized differently, part of a different subculture, vulnerable to different social pressures, or aspiring to different goals than less aggressive people? The remaining five suggestions apply to questions for any discipline, not just sociology.

Ask a question that requires more than a simple *yes* or *no* answer. A "yes–no" question is a dead end. The case is already closed and there is nothing to investigate or argue. For example, the question "Does socioeconomic status affect marital stability?" can be answered "yes," and there is no more to say. The same with this question: "Can children born with severe language/communication deficits caused by aphasia be socialized to participate in society on a par with nonaphasic persons?" One way to improve such questions is to put the phrase "To what extent . . ." in front of them. For example, "To what extent do socioeconomic statuses affect marital stability?" Another remedy is to rephrase the question. For example, "What are the most effective ways for primary schools to enhance the normal socialization of children born with severe language/communication deficits caused by aphasia?"

Ask a question that has more than one plausible answer. The paper's task is to demonstrate why your answer is more valid than other plausible answers. "Do social conditions affect the crime rate?" is not a genuine question because *no* is not a plausible answer. "Are crime rates more sensitive to economic inequality or differences in family structure?" is a better question because you will find sociologists arguing for both answers. Belaboring the obvious wastes time. Before starting the research, address different plausible answers to your question. Can you imagine anyone seriously defending the other side? If not, you need to reformulate the question.

Unless your assignment specifies otherwise, ask a question that draws relationships between two or more concepts. Exceptions to this are a definition paper, a "feeling" or reaction paper, and a story or narrative paper. Typically, sociological questions pose something to be explained, which is the dependent variable (for example, why do some people become criminals?). Then the author makes a case, such as people who are raised in dysfunctional families or people with criminal friends are more likely to commit crimes than others. This is the independent variable. The point is a sound sociological paper is usually based on something to be explained. Unless specifically instructed, avoid questions that address only one concept, such as "What is deviance?"

Make sure you have access to the information needed to answer your question. Although some paper assignments do not require any research outside assigned readings and lectures, many require you to document your points with evidence. For these papers, you must consider whether you can realistically get the necessary documentation. For example, "Has deviance always existed?" is an interesting question with important consequences for sociological theory. But it would be difficult to document adequately whether prehistoric societies had deviance. Still, you may be surprised at what information does exist and how easily it can be located with a little effort.

Make sure your question is answerable in the space allowed. Staying within the paper's required parameters can be difficult given the vast amount of information available. It is essential to stay focused on your question and follow your outline.

SUMMING UP

Many students feel that sociology helps them see the world in a whole new way, like the fish that pokes its head into the air and notices that it has been in water all this time. The most fundamental part of the sociological worldview is learning to ask questions you never would have thought of previously—questions that probe the ways society affects individuals, questions that seek patterns in how people do things together, questions that connect individual biographies to the panorama of history. Writing the best sociological papers begins with asking sociological questions. Admittedly it is not always easy because most students intuitively think in individualistic terms. But the rewards are worth the effort. Asking a sound sociological question guides you toward writing an outstanding sociological paper. Not only will it help you get a better grade, it will help you more clearly understand the world.

Designing Your Paper

You don't start out writing good stuff. You start out writing crap and thinking it's good stuff, and then gradually you get better at it. That's why I say one of the most valuable traits is persistence.

OCTAVIA E. BUTLER

In the "Information Age" facts are easy to come by. Most college students can readily find out the biggest grossing film of 2012. But for many, developing a coherent, logical argument that combines theoretical insight and empirical support—the skills that college is supposed to teach—can be a real challenge. Design is the connection between abstract conception and concrete execution, just as the blueprint is the link between imagination and actually building a house. This chapter is about the big picture of paper writing—how the pieces fit together (structure), how to connect conclusions to evidence (logic), how to make sense of the whole. We focus on the elements of structure and highlight some of the "shoulds" and "should nots" of logic. We clarify some important terms professors commonly use in essay assignments and exams. Further, we discuss how to write an effective paper proposal.

DEVELOPING AN ARGUMENT: LOGIC AND STRUCTURE

In writing, logic refers to the relationship between the paper's assertions and its evidence. Structure concerns how the parts of the paper fit together. According to one faculty survey, logic and structure are among the most important criteria instructors weigh in grading papers.

Logic demands that a good paper go beyond mere assertion ("This statement is true because I say it is"). The answer to your paper's question, discussed in the last chapter, is your *thesis*. To be convincing, your thesis must be supported by evidence and reasoning. One way to accomplish this is to assume the reader is naive or skeptical. Try to imagine actively what a naive reader might not understand about what you are saying and explain your points to him or her. Try to imagine the kind of doubts a skeptic might hold and attempt to convince him or her, just like a debater would.

Structure demands that each sentence should be well written and be logical. Each sentence should be logically connected to the sentences around it, each paragraph to the paragraphs around it, each section to the section around it, and all of them connected to the overall theme of the paper. By the time you submit your paper, you should be able to conceptualize the structure of the paper in your head and explain that structure to the instructor, if necessary. This means being able to state in one or two sentences what your paper's main thesis is and how you go about arguing that thesis. Imagine your roommate or a friend asking "What's the point of the paper?" and "Why should the reader believe you?" If you can't answer those questions, you still have work to do before turning in the final draft.

Once you have framed your question and developed your thesis you will begin constructing a logical defense of your thesis—why your answer is more correct than alternative answers. This defense requires evidence that supports your thesis. The evidence must be logically connected to the thesis so you can make the statement: "If the evidence is true, the thesis is true." Many student papers and some professional papers falter here, presenting interesting and important evidence in narrative form, or in a controlled study, or sometimes through reasoned reflection, but then drawing a weak conclusion. So be sure to put aside the actual paper and review the first three items on the checklist presented in Part 4: "What is my thesis? Does my thesis remain clear and central throughout the paper? Have I supported my thesis with adequate evidence?"

THE ELEMENTS OF STRUCTURE: INTRODUCTIONS, TRANSITIONS, AND CONCLUSIONS

The structure of the paper should reflect the logical connection of the evidence to the thesis. It is the writer's job to draw the connections between evidence and conclusions and to show how the paper logically proceeds. Thus the paper's introduction, transitions, and conclusions are essential, not just incidental, parts of the paper. The *introduction* should state the question and specify the plan for answering it. Introductions are difficult because the writer is making a transition from nothing to something. A good introduction should capture the reader's attention. Many writers achieve this by presenting an anecdote about an individual or event, offering a pithy quotation relevant to the topic, asking a question, or beginning with a broad issue and then focusing on the specific topic of the paper. A preview of the paper is also helpful.

As the paper unfolds, provide guideposts or *transitions* for the reader reviewing what the paper has covered and previewing what to expect next. These transitions indicate how sentences, paragraphs, and sections logically fit together. Transitions can be accomplished by including transitional words and phrases, such as "on the other hand" and "furthermore." (See Chapter 3 for a list of transitions.) They can also be stated in sentences: "The last section discussed Durkheim's basic presuppositions; this section will show how those presuppositions influenced his theory of religion." A common writing error is the *non sequitur,* a Latin phrase for sentences or paragraphs that have no apparent connection. This often results from a connection that is in the writer's mind but that fails to be demonstrated to the reader with transition sentences.

Unless your instructor says otherwise, most papers should be broken down into different sections, each marked by a section heading. The kind of sections depends on the type of paper. A quantitative paper should begin with an unmarked introduction; followed by sections called Literature Review, Methods, and Results; and end with a discussion. A paper about a sociological theorist might have sections on different stages of the theorist's life or different major themes. Generally, a paper should have no more than three major sections plus an introduction and conclusion. Sometimes sections can have subsections, depending on the type of paper, size, and instructor preference.

A *conclusion* should remind readers where they have been and how the thesis has been demonstrated. Try to summarize the paper without repeating specific sentences. This is also the appropriate place to reflect upon the larger implications of your thesis—to answer the question "So what?" But it is not appropriate to present new evidence in the conclusion.

LOGICAL FALLACIES

One of the best ways to examine the relationship between logic and evidence is to review common logical fallacies. Logical fallacies are errors in reasoning and can lead writers to inappropriate conclusions. Try to avoid the following typical errors:

+ **ad hominem:** Attacking or praising the opponent's character, not the issue. It is illogical to reject or support an argument based on who said it, no matter how legitimate the criticism or admiration. For example, "They believe that animals have 'inherent moral rights.' But some of the people who most vigorously support animal rights are cruel to their own family members." Even if some animal rights advocates are cruel to their own family members (and we are not suggesting they are), that would not be logical evidence against their arguments about animal rights.
+ **circular reasoning:** This means that two parts of a statement each depend on the other. For example, "If stealing was legal, then it wouldn't be prohibited by the law." That statement assumes what it is trying to prove. Thus the reasoning goes in a circle.
+ **false dilemma:** In a statement that should offer alternative choices, there is only one given choice, or two or more choices that are exclusive.

In the statement "If school reforms in the last several decades have not created high-quality education for everyone, it is time for school vouchers." High-quality education and school vouchers are not incompatible but it is logically possible that high-quality education could come with or without school vouchers, as well as other alternatives.

+ **false analogy:** Assuming that because people or objects share one characteristic, they share all characteristics. Analogy can be a very important source of sociological information. Finding the similarities between race and gender has been a major advance in knowledge. But it does not follow that everything about being a woman is the same as being an African American, even if there are similarities.

+ **false cause,** also called *post hoc, ergo propter hoc:* Assuming that because one thing happened after another, it is caused by the first event. If a writer wanted to demonstrate that "After people lost respect for government authority in the 1960s, violent crime rose all across the country," it would have to provide evidence for a causal link between the loss of respect for authority and the rise in violent crime. Timing alone does not prove causality.

+ **sweeping generalization:** This error is especially tempting because sociologists are expected to draw large conclusions from specific facts. They are supposed to ask "So what?" But it is important to ask whether the generalization follows the finding. A paper might claim that "Recent polls about attitudes toward government funding of health care confirm that Americans will never accept a single-payer medical insurance system." But generalizations about the future based on polls about the present cannot be justified.

+ **non sequitur:** Making no logical conclusion. All statements that follow an if-then logic, whether or not explicitly using the terms "if" and "then," must make a legitimate logical connection. The "then" must be truly based on the "if." The premise in the "if" clause must lead to the claim in the "then" premise. A paper that claimed "If stress factors lead to a weakening of willpower causing binge eating, then all diet centers should provide counseling sessions" would not be justified. The premise is in the "if" clause—that stress factors can weaken willpower and spark binge eating—but there is no logical connection to the "then" conclusion—that diet centers should provide counseling sessions. It might be true that diet centers should provide counseling sessions, but we would need more sound reasoning from other facts to know.

+ **reverse reasoning:** Confusing cause for effect. For example, "The more knowledge teenagers have about sex, the more likely they are to engage in premarital sexual activities." Sorting out cause and effect is one of the enduring challenges of sociology. For example, a survey might show that teenagers who have premarital sex are more knowledgeable about sex than those who don't. It would be wrong to conclude that the knowledge about sex is the cause of sexual activity when it is just as likely to be the opposite—that knowledge of sex comes from sexual activity.

✦ **slippery slope:** An argument offers a causal chain containing weak links. For example, "If we ban smoking, then people will start taking soft drugs and then move on to hard drugs, and then the crime rate will increase. Therefore, we should prevent crime by allowing smoking."

✦ **spurious causation:** Treating things with a common cause as though they affect each other. Spurious causations occur when we have two correlated events. When one of them changes, we typically expect the other to change; however, while we may be tempted to assume that one causes the other, we must look for a third variable that produces the correlation between the two events. For example, someone might determine that drowning deaths in public swimming pools are caused by increased ice cream consumption. Although it is true that the rate of drowning deaths and the rate of ice cream consumption both increase together, this is not a causal relationship. Instead, both are caused by a third variable: warm weather.

For a fuller description of logical errors, see David Hackett Fischer, *Historians' Fallacies: Toward a Logic of Historical Thought* (1970. New York: Harper & Row). Even though written specifically for historians, it is very useful for all writers.

TWO FORMATS OF LOGIC AND STRUCTURE

We suggest two formats of logic and structure that are common in sociology papers. However, there are other formats that may be appropriate for specific assignments. If the paper assignment does not specify an explicit format requirement, discuss your format ideas with the instructor.

The Three-Part Essay Format This type of paper is most commonly structured in terms of a major thesis and three supporting points.

There is nothing magical about the number three; it is a convenient number of points for the length and scope of papers typically written for course assignments. Each of the three points should logically support the thesis. You should be able to say "if point A (or B, or C) is true, the thesis is true." In terms of formal logic, you need to be able to maintain that "if point A (or B, or C) were *not* true, the thesis would probably not be true."

For example, consider the thesis: "Over the last hundred years, educational opportunities in America have opened up the American social structure to more upward mobility."

Point A could be: Educational achievement is more closely connected to high-status jobs than it was a hundred years ago.

Point B could be: Education is more equally accessible to all members of the society than were earlier means of achieving social status.

Point C could be: The content of education relates more to job skills than it did a hundred years ago.

The paper itself is structured around an introduction, discussion of point A, discussion of point B, discussion of point C, and a conclusion. The introduction presents the question that is being answered, the general thesis, and usually a plan for the body of the paper. Each point is discussed in turn. Each section usually starts with a claim—a statement of its main point. Often the next sentence is an example of this claim, followed by an explanation of how the example illustrates the point. Then you can elaborate on this point, identify its implications, take issue with some aspects, or provide other types of evidence. Finally, you need to tie it back in with your general thesis and argument.

You will need at least one paragraph for each discussion section; you may need more than one paragraph to discuss each main point, especially if the point is complicated or you are presenting elaborate evidence. If so, allocate separate paragraphs to each subpoint or aspect. The discussion gives evidence and reasoning for why the point is true; the discussion also explains the logical connection between that point and the general thesis. The conclusion then summarizes the overall argument and often offers your personal thoughts about the issue.

A modified version of the essay format is also appropriate for a paper based on ethnographic research. For an ethnographic research paper, follow the structure described in this section, replacing the thesis and supporting claims with three major themes, or three points about a single theme, gathered from your data. See Chapter 9 for details on this modified application.

The Journal Format This is the format often found in articles in major academic journals such as the *American Sociological Review* and the *American Journal of Sociology*. The journal format is not the same as journalistic style. Journalistic style is sometimes used to describe the easy and fluid style of writing in popular magazines such as *TIME*. The journal format refers to a particular way that a paper or article can be organized. Rarely would the journalistic style of writing be used in a paper organized in the journal format. The journal format follows the procedural logic of the hypothesis testing mode of conducting research, in which you formally test a specific hypothesis through systematic research. Although usable for projects other than formal hypothesis testing, it is best suited for projects that include systematic data collection and analysis and is structured as follows: introduction (including the literature review and the statement of hypothesis), methods, results, and discussion. (See Chapter 8 on the quantitative research paper, for more detail.)

The introduction specifies the question that is being answered. In this section, a review of the literature summarizes what other people have written about the topic, explaining why it is an important issue to study and what their answers are. It is important that the literature review not be a laundry list of "he said, she said" but a logical assessment of what is known and not known about your question. This section should also formally state your

> *"What's important is the way we say it. Art is all about craftsmanship. Others can interpret craftsmanship as style if they wish. Style is what unites memory or recollection, ideology, sentiment, nostalgia, presentiment, to the way we express all that. It's not what we say but how we say it that matters."*
>
> Federico Fellini

hypothesis (for example, "A greater proportion of men today hold higher status jobs than their fathers did a hundred years ago) and justify why you expect it to be true. We will discuss the review of the literature in more depth in Chapter 8.

The methods section reports your research procedure, detailing where you found the data, how the variables were measured, and what sort of analysis you conducted on the data. A reader should be able to replicate your study by following the guidelines in your methods section.

The results section reports in literal terms what the study shows. For instance, "30 percent of men one hundred years ago were in higher-status jobs than their fathers, while 29 percent of men today are in higher-status jobs than their fathers," which is virtually no change. (These numbers are made up for this book. They are not accurate.)

The discussion section draws the conclusions and reflects upon the results (see Chapter 8). For example: "The hypothesis must be rejected. The Occupational structure has not opened up. The American promise of equal chance for all is not yet fulfilled."

The essay and journal formats are illustrated by sample student papers in this book. The sample paper on quantitative research (see Chapter 8) follows the journal format. The other three sample papers—one based on textual analysis (see Chapter 6), one based on library research (see Chapter 7), and another demonstrating ethnographic field research (see Chapter 9)—are modified versions of the essay format.

TERMS AND STRATEGIES IN ESSAY AND EXAM ASSIGNMENTS

When students are given a writing assignment, an instructor often uses terms that seem general or abstract but may have a precise academic meaning. Knowing the course content may not be enough to do well on a paper assignment if the student misunderstands what is being asked; knowing *what to do* with this content and having a strategy for selecting and presenting this information are essential. The way to determine such an appropriate strategy is to scrutinize the wording of the assignment, to clarify for yourself what is expected, and then to use a suitable strategy to produce the paper.

Instructors deliberately design assignments to encourage you to work with course concepts and data in various ways. For example, writing about deviance could involve defining it, illustrating it, analyzing it, comparing it with other behavior, evaluating its effects, summarizing theories about it, etc. Sometimes instructors will provide you with a well-framed, clear question to start with. At the other extreme, you may be given a vague assignment, such as "discuss deviance," that will require you to create and frame your own question. In the middle of this range are common commands listed below that cue you to appropriate questions about the course information.

They also tell you what the instructor wants you to do with this information. Analytic concepts that are often used casually outside of the academic context have very specific sociological meanings. Students need to be aware of what these terms mean so they don't misunderstand the assignment.

Analyze: Break something down into its parts; for example, a theory into its components, a process into its stages, an event into its causes. Analysis involves characterizing the whole, identifying the parts, and showing how the parts relate to one another to make the whole. Corresponding question: "What is the relationship of goals and opportunities in Merton's theory of deviance?"

Assess/Criticize/Evaluate: Determine the importance or value of something. Assessing requires you to develop clearly stated criteria of judgment and to comment on the elements that meet or fail to meet those criteria. Corresponding question: "How useful is labeling theory for explaining why people join gangs?"

Classify: Sort something into main categories and thereby pigeonhole its parts. Corresponding question: "If someone cheats on an examination to get a better grade, which of Merton's forms of deviance does the behavior belong to?"

Compare/Contrast: Identify the important similarities and differences between two elements in order to reveal something significant about them. Emphasize similarities if the command is to compare, and differences if it is to contrast. Corresponding question: "What are the similarities and differences between labeling theory and Merton's theories of deviance?"

Define/Identify: Give the special characteristics by which a concept, thing, or event can be recognized; that is, what it is and what it is not. Defining is more than just describing a word's essence. You should also place it in its general class and then distinguish it from other members of that class. Corresponding questions: "What is anomie? What behaviors or attitudes indicate that a person or group is anomic?"

Describe: Present the characteristics by which an object, action, person, or concept can be recognized or an event or process can be visualized. Corresponding question: "What is Merton's theory of deviance?"

Discuss/Examine: Analyze and/or evaluate a particular topic. You must decide on your own a question concerning the things to be discussed. Instructors usually expect you to go beyond summary. Corresponding question: "What can sociological theories tell us about why gangs exist and why individuals join them?"

Explain/Justify: Make clear the reasons for or the basic principles of something; make it intelligible. Explanation may involve relating the unfamiliar to the more familiar. Corresponding questions: "Why do people break rules that they believe in? What theories do you think give the best explanation of this kind of behavior? What evidence can you present to support these theories?"

Illustrate: Use a concrete example to explain or clarify the fundamental attributes of a problem or concept. Corresponding question: "Give a concrete example of 'innovative deviance.' How does this example show the defining features of the concept?"

Interpret: Explain what the author of a quotation means. Restate what the author said and go beyond, saying something more about his or her ideas. Corresponding question: "What does Durkheim mean by stating that animals cannot commit suicide?"

List/Enumerate: Give essential points one by one in a logical order. Corresponding question: "What are the forms of deviance in Merton's theory of deviance?"

Outline/Trace/Review/State: Organize a description under main points and subordinate points, omitting minor details and stressing the classification of the elements of the problem or the main points in the development of an event or issue. Corresponding questions: "What have been the major debates over deviance in the past quarter century? How has the resolution of one debate led into the next? Highlight these debates with reference to leading theories and pathbreaking studies."

Prove/Validate: Establish that something is true by citing factual evidence or giving clear, logical reasons for believing it is true. Corresponding question: "Make a case on behalf of or in opposition to labeling theory. What is the strongest justification and best evidence you can present to support your point of view?"

Note that sometimes an assignment calls for more than one question because the instructor combines these commands, thereby requiring you to work with the material in several ways. At other times, instructors provide several versions of essentially the same question but repeat it in different words to help you understand what you are supposed to do. If your assignment seems to call for several questions, first determine whether they are the same question restated differently or whether they involve separate strategies.

ANSWERING AN ESSAY EXAM QUESTION

Because essay exams test thinking, not the ability to memorize details, understanding the directions represented by the terms just listed is especially important. This is particularly true when you are writing under time pressure. Instructors want to see the big picture—meaningful generalizations—in your exam essay. They want you demonstrate quickly what all the details covered in class add up to. To put it another way, they want you to show that you can see the forest for the trees. Because instructors differ in whether they prefer depth or breadth, you should ask your instructor how much analysis or detail is expected. Therefore, answering an instructor's ready-made question requires a special approach.

Begin by reading through the exam sheet(s) **twice** in order to make choices, if they are available, and to ration your time. Otherwise, you may confuse the number of questions or not understand important directions. Start with the question you feel most confident about answering, even if it's not in the first section of the exam. (Be sure to label the number of each question as you answer it.) Other ideas will come to you as you write, and your relatively easy answer will build your confidence.

Underline or circle the key terms, like "analyze," "evaluate," "how" or "in what way," and "how much" or "to what extent." If the instructions simply say "discuss," you're on your own. Are there several theorists, institutions, or concepts, for example, that pertain to the question? Try a *comparison.* Does the question require demonstrated understanding of key terms? Try *defining* and *illustrating.* Is a process important? Try *analyzing* its different stages. Would grouping help? Try *classification.*

One common essay-exam strategy is to begin by cannibalizing the words in the question and using them as a ready-made part of your thesis answer. For example:

> *Question:* "In what ways has the subsequent development of the West confirmed or disconfirmed Marx's theory about class conflict in capitalism?"

> *Answer:* "The subsequent development of the West has disconfirmed Marx's theory about class conflict in capitalism in at least three ways. First, the class structure did not polarize into two unbridgeable classes, but instead gave rise to a very large middle class. Second, life chances for wealth and prestige now depend at least as much on education and occupation as on class background. Third, the revolutions Marx predicted in advanced capitalist societies did not occur, but instead have developed primarily in peasant-based societies."

Such a bald statement might be too obvious for a polished *paper,* but for an exam essay, an announcement like this can help you outline your answer.

Focusing on the question is essential. The object of your essay is **not** to demonstrate all the facts you know, but to answer the question as clearly and concisely as possible.

THE PROPOSAL

A *proposal,* sometimes called a "statement of intent," is a preview of your paper. Instructors assign a proposal to get you started on your paper by framing a question and making a commitment to answering it with evidence from either textual analysis, library research, quantitative research, or qualitative research. Even though a proposal may not lead to a finished paper, it can be a useful learning experience. As the first stage in a full paper, it helps you focus on how to ask questions and plan the other stages. It is also a useful skill for professional life. Most professional jobs require writing proposals at some point, whether to compete for resources or to design a course of action. Obviously, your proposal can't describe your intended paper in much detail because at this stage you often don't know much about the topic. However, you can frame your question and provide a context for it. As such, the proposal is a quick introduction, often only one or two pages long, about what you want to do. Your instructor can advise you about possible leads to follow or alert you to potential problems.

Your proposal should feature your research question. For example, "To what extent is homelessness attributable to mental illness?" Additionally, it may include any of the following, depending on what you already know or hope to discover:

- **an academic justification for studying this topic:** that is, why it interests other researchers. Does it provide an opportunity to illustrate, test, or compare one or more sociological theories? Or does the topic have substantive, practical, or policy implications? For example, "What does the increasing problem of urban homelessness mean for policymakers, for providers of social services, for public health and recreation, for tourism, and for others in addition to the homeless people themselves?"

- **related questions** triggered by your main question, such as: "What counts as mental illness?" and "Who counts as homeless?" These questions must be considered when operationally defining your variables in a quantitative paper. The question "Which comes first: the illness or the homelessness?" is related to the causal order you specify in a quantitative paper. "What drives people onto the streets?" "How do people survive in these conditions?" "Where do homeless people go for help?" "Why do some people get off the street while others don't?" These are alternative questions you may want to investigate rather than the one you originally planned to answer.

- **a provisional answer** to your question: in other words, your thesis (or hypothesis, if you're doing a quantitative research paper). An example of a thesis might be: "Many older homeless people behave eccentrically, but increasingly children and families are being made homeless and they are not necessarily mentally ill, at least not before becoming homeless." An example of a hypothesis might be: "As unemployment rates increase, the number of homeless people increases." These provisional answers may be just hunches or "educated guesses" based on course materials. You will definitely refine your thesis or hypothesis as you learn more about your topic, and in the process you may change it entirely.

- **a method for answering the question:** if you are doing a library research paper, you need to state what you will find out first (for example, reputable estimates on how many homeless people there are) and where you will start looking for it. If you are doing a quantitative research paper, your instructor will want a detailed methodological blueprint with a step-by-step plan listing variables, or, for a qualitative research paper, a description of the ethnographic site where you will be making observations. You need to demonstrate that what you plan to do will provide an adequate answer to your question. This sometimes will require acknowledging the limitations of your answer. For example, "We really don't know exactly how many homeless people there are because they are difficult to identify. Moreover, some types of mental illness, such as paranoid schizophrenia, are easier to detect than equally debilitating forms, such as severe depression." What this means is that you need to do preliminary reading and thinking before you write your proposal.

A SAMPLE STUDENT PROPOSAL

Here is a sample proposal for a quantitative research paper, using a journal format, that student Christina De Roulhac wrote for an Honor's Thesis. The assignment was to identify a research question, set it within an academic context, and outline a way to answer that question. One of the admirable qualities of this proposal is that she takes a very controversial issue in which emotions often overshadow information and identifies a question that can be answered by research. She does not claim to have no opinion, and she alerts the reader that her family has been very active in the church. The structure of this proposal is very straightforward. Christina states a question nearly everyone can relate to, specifies it in sociological terms, offers a hypothesis of what she thinks the answer is, cites the sociological basis of that answer, describes a method for answering the question, gives a caveat about her personal involvement in the study, and reminds the reader why the issue is important. Not all proposals have to fit this model, but it is a useful template.

OUR COMMENTS

Christina De Roulhac

Sociology 191
January 9, 2006

PROPOSAL

In the present debate over homosexuality, some pastors and churches actively uphold traditional Biblical interpretations regarding same sex relations, while others challenge these teachings and welcome gay, lesbian, bisexual, and transgender individuals as well as advocate for their rights. Using the current controversy over homosexuality in American Baptist Churches (ABC) USA, a mainline protestant Christian denomination, I will study when and how pastors and churches encourage liberalism and when and how pastors and churches promote conservatism. Liberalism is a Protestant movement that favors free intellectual inquiry, stresses the ethical and humanitarian content of Christianity, and de-emphasizes dogmatic theology. In contrast, conservatism is a theological orientation that aims to maintain the existing or traditional order. This issue is particularly salient in ABC because the Pacific Southwest, an ABC region of about 300 churches, decided on May 11, 2006, to sever ties with ABC over irresolvable differences in Biblical interpretation, particularly in regards to homosexuality.

My hypothesis is that a mutual and reciprocal influence between Biblical interpretation and a church's desired niche in the Christian marketplace leads a number of pastors and churches to encourage liberalism and other pastors and churches to promote conservatism.

My hypothesis builds upon the economic and sociological model of the Christian marketplace that "views churches and their clergy as religious producers who choose the characteristics of their product and the means

1

The question is inspired more by a topical issue than sociological theory, but it is framed in such a way that empirical research will provide an objective answer. Empirical research is based on the collection of data using methods such as structured observation, archival analysis, survey, or experiment.

The two major concepts, *liberalism* and *conservatism,* are defined.

This is a clear hypothesis stated in a way that can be tested to determine if it is true, though there is a hint of tautology. *Tautology* is a statement that is true by definition. The study would be tautological if Christina used their support or condemnation of homosexuality as evidence of what their desire was.

> The hypothesis is drawn from sociological theory, not her own preconceptions. She could have clarified how the theory might have to be reevaluated if the hypothesis does not hold up. Would it have to be slightly modified or reconsidered as an entire theory?

of marketing it. Consumers in turn choose what religion, if any, they will accept and how extensively they will participate in it." (Finke and Iannaccone 1993:28). In this model, pastors and churches must meet consumers' demand in order to survive, but also play a role in creating new niches and markets. The "niche" is also an important concept because it is "a way of specifying competitive processes and environmental dependencies" in an environment, such as the Christian marketplace (Hannan, Carroll, and Polos 2003:309).

My hypothesis also builds upon N. J. Demerath's (1995) "Cultural Victory and Organizational Defeat in the Paradoxical Decline of Liberal Protestantism," which asserts that fulfilling a niche in the Christian market is important, especially for liberal churches. Demerath argues that the liberal Protestant values of individualism, freedom, pluralism, tolerance, democracy, and intellectual inquiry are related to decreased membership relative to more conservative, strict churches. To offset their disadvantage, Demerath (1995) suggests that the liberal churches that thrive fill particular niches because they are "groups that have coalesced successfully around distinctive liberal political agendas (whether pro–civil rights, antipoverty, or antiwar), and those strict liberal congregations whose solidarity derives from a bold identification with a distinctive lifestyle—e.g., gay and lesbian" (p. 466). Both liberal and conservative pastors and churches make decisions and act in a way that preserves their place in a desired niche, and these decisions influence and are influenced by Biblical interpretation.

> This is a clear description of her sample. If the proposal had been longer, she might have added more detail about how they would be found and recruited.

For this study I will interview 10–16 pastors from ABC, who represent different points in the homosexuality debate. Half the pastors will be liberal and welcoming and affirming of gays in the church, and the other half of the pastors will be more conservative in their views. I will ask how they got involved in the homosexuality debate, how their Biblical interpretation effects the decisions they make for the church, and why they think people

> This should be "affects." It is a very common error to confuse "affect" and "effect."

2

choose to join their church. The interviews with pastors will be supplemented by interviews with new members of the represented churches. In these interviews I will ask why they joined this particular church and what they think of their church's stance on the issue of homosexuality.

My family's involvement in ABC is both a strength and limitation of this research. It is a strength because I have connections to many pastors, but a weakness because I have my own views in this debate. My views will not influence my research because I will not be studying the arguments of each side of the debate, but instead I will study the factors that precipitate and fuel pastors' and churches' decisions and actions. This research is important because the issue of homosexuality is a widespread controversy in many mainline Protestant denominations as well as politics in the United States.

REFERENCES

Demerath, N. J. 1995. "Cultural Victory and Organizational Defeat in the Paradoxical Decline of Liberal Protestantism." *Journal for the Scientific Study of Religion* 34:458–69.

Finke, Roger and Laurence Iannaccone. 1993. "Supply-Side Explanations for Religious Change." Pp. 27–39 in *Annals of the American Academy of Political and Social Science,* vol. 527, *Religion in the Nineties,* edited by W. C. Roof. Thousand Oaks, CA: SAGE Publications.

Hannan, Michael, Glenn Carroll, and Laszlo Polos. 2003. "The Organizational Niche." *Sociological Theory* 21:309–340.

What the proposal needs at this point is specification of how the interview data would be used to accept or reject her hypotheses. How would she know whether the pastors were sensitive to niches and whether their knowledge of niches affected their attitude toward homosexuality? How would she reject a more conventional explanation that ministers preach what they believe and that parishioners either stay or leave depending on whether they agree?

Although the larger social implications of this topic are obvious, it is a good idea to point them out.

According to the most recent edition of the *American Sociological Association Style Guide* (2010), references to journal articles should include the issue number after the volume number.

THE WRITING PROCESS

I told students that it didn't make much difference what they wrote in a first draft because they could always change it. Since what they put on a piece of paper was not necessarily final, they needn't worry so much about what they wrote. The only version that mattered was the last one.

HOWARD S. BECKER
Writing for Social Scientists

THE SECRET TO WRITING IS WRITING

The secret to writing is writing, rewriting, and writing again. To produce finished writing, every writer has to put pencil to scratch pad, pen to paper, fingers to keyboard—in some way the writer's words must be inscribed in marks that can be read by readers and reread by the writer.

How easy or difficult the process of writing is for the writer often depends more on the context for writing than on the specific talents of the writer. When our messages are relatively simple and our writing is unlikely to be judged critically, writing can be quick and easy: think Facebook, Twitter, or e-mail. But when we are writing about complex topics in relatively high-stakes contexts with grades, reputation, even potential jobs and income on the line, writing can be much more difficult. Even experienced writers procrastinate and develop writer's block. And yet, they *want* to write. How then does writing ever get done? Writers often engage in an all-night marathon of writing just completed before a pressing deadline. But the product of this painful process of avoidance and panicky composition at the last moment is rarely the writer's best work and often does not earn the evaluation—the grade, the positive comments, the feeling of accomplishment—that writers hope for.

Few people actually have extended periods for writing. Successful writers learn to make time to write by breaking down complex writing tasks like completing a publishable article or an "A" paper into smaller chunks they can work on over days, weeks, or months—they develop a process for writing.

"The scariest moment is always just before you start."

Stephen King
On Writing

All the steps that go into a final paper or textbook chapter or journal article are invisible. Usually we only see someone else's final product; however, no one ever sits down, thinks, and then types an "A" paper all at once. Writing is *not* a delivery system of ready-made ideas. Every good writer goes through a process—doodles an outline, a provisional question or list of questions, a thesis, hypothesis or an easy paragraph. Then the writer reviews it, likes some aspects, and considers how to develop those aspects or considers what additional information is needed and does more reading; or the writer sees logical gaps and works to make the argument more coherent. Additionally, the writer may dislike the way some sentences sound and decide to rewrite them or rearrange paragraphs to enhance the flow or logic of the paper. This recursive process continues and may encourage or develop further ideas.

There is no one right way to move through the stages of the writing process. For example, some people prefer writing down everything that occurs to them about the general topic. Then they search through it for threads of thought and possibilities, and later outline the previously disorganized ideas. Other writers work out a highly structured outline first because the logical subdivisions help them understand potential relationships between ideas. Then they compose a draft, possibly beginning to write sentences and paragraphs about ideas somewhere in the middle or at the end of their outline. The act of writing often triggers more ideas, so you may find that outlining comes easier after you've written some ideas or after your first rough draft.

While we are not recommending any one particular way to navigate through the stages of this writing and rewriting process, we would like to offer suggestions for drafting your paper—particularly ways of getting started and the value of outlining and revising.

STRATEGIES FOR GETTING STARTED

As stated earlier, some students are surprised to learn that even the most successful writers experience writing anxiety. Writers feel vulnerable when their inner thoughts and facility with written language are on public display. They recall negative comments about their writing more easily than positive ones and they may anticipate criticism as they struggle to find the best words to convey their ideas. It is important to acknowledge the anxiety of writing and begin writing anyway. Some people may find talking to a friend or a professional at your school's writing center or counseling center beneficial. While we cannot offer easy solutions for writing anxiety, this section suggests ways to overcome it.

GETTING IDEAS

The first steps in any type of writing involve generating initial ideas and making decisions about the form the writing will take. These initial steps may be intimidating when writers feel stressed by time constraints or unfamiliarity with the genre and content of their work. Taking action when a project is first assigned can save time in the long run by getting your writing process started in the right direction. Some useful steps to begin include:

+ Review your assignment carefully. What does the instructor want? Instructors may not always specify their expectations, so if you are unsure about what to write, make an appointment to see your instructor early in the writing process. Don't expect the instructor to generate ideas for you. Bring in notes, an outline, or a rough proposal. Try to ask specific questions about how you should proceed with the assignment. Some of the hardest feelings about grading result from a good paper getting a low grade because a student misread the assignment.

+ Gather initial ideas. Review your class notes, rereading relevant parts of assigned reading. Browse online academic resources from your library or through search engines like Google Scholar to get an overview of issues involved with your question. Note key words that identify major concepts you may need for further research.

+ Do some private writing. For the moment, forget about being graded or otherwise critiqued. Generate ideas by thinking out loud on paper. No one else needs to see your writing. You can later choose which ideas you want to present to others. Try some of the following techniques:

    + **Freewriting.** This is brainstorming or free association. Just write nonstop for 5–15 minutes with no censoring of your ideas. At the end of 15 minutes review your writing to find key words or phrases you like, underline them, and then immediately add 5–15 minutes more of writing. Continue to underline key words and phrases you can use in later writing.

    + **Lists.** Jot down all the ideas or questions that you associate with or might need for your paper, then group them into families and number each group, creating a possible sequence for your paper.

    + **Reporter's Notebook.** Consider the journalism questions "Who?" "What?" "Where" "When?" "Why?" and "How?" and try to create information related to the general topic for each question.

    + **Diagrams.** Some people are visually oriented and like seeing their ideas emerging as pictures on the page. Here are several different kinds of diagrams you can try:

        + *Clustering.* Write one key word or phrase (for example, a person's name, an issue, a term) in the middle of a sheet of paper. Circle it and then write down related concepts and examples in their own circles elsewhere on the page. Draw lines between the circles to indicate various logical relationships between the items.

        + *Branching.* Build a tree from a key word or phrase. Analyze it into its branch ideas and then into the twig and leaf ideas. Your tree can be vertical, horizontal, or upside down.

"Writing is an exploration. You start from nothing and learn as you go."

E.L. Doctorow

+ *Columns.* Set up a compare-and-contrast table in two columns. In each column include the information that fits under the items you are juxtaposing.
+ *Flow chart.* Put your major concepts (or variables) in boxes with causes (or independent variables) on the left side of the page, effects (or dependent variables) on the right, and mediating processes (or intervening variables) in between. Draw lines and arrows between the boxes to show causal relationships. This is an excellent technique to keep information clear and organized.

+ Talk about your ideas. Explaining your developing argument to other students in your class or study group helps generate new ideas. If your school has a writing center, make an appointment early in your writing process to meet with one of their staff. Writing center staff are experienced in helping students develop and organize ideas.

OUTLINING

Once you have generated ideas, creating a formal outline may be helpful even before beginning your paper. Writing an outline can provide at least two benefits at different stages in the writing process: it can give birth to ideas and it can describe the connections between ideas that are already articulated. An informal outline is the product of idea-generating techniques like those described above; a formal outline is a blueprint or a road map that tracks the relationship and sequence of main ideas in your paper. An informal outline is private; its purpose is discovery, not presentation to others. A formal outline can be shown to an instructor before the paper's due date to ensure you're on target. It is much easier to revise an outline by adding, eliminating, or shifting main parts than it is to repair a completed paper.

A formal outline is a completed set of ideas, arranged in a specific sequence. It can be a topic outline composed of words and phrases like a table of contents, or it can be a sentence outline. In either case, a proper presentation outline signals the order and relationship of ideas through visual layout (headings and indentations) and through a symbol system, either an alternating number-letter system (roman numeral, capital letter, Arabic numeral, lowercase letter) or a number system (1, 1.1, 1.1.2, etc.).

For example, student Dana E. Knickerbocker began with this question: "How does gender affect capital-punishment sentencing?" Dana's next step was to outline three alternative answers:

1. The "chivalry" theory indicates that gender bias in capital sentencing works to a woman's advantage.
2. The "evil woman" theory proposes that the relatively few women who do receive capital sentences have violated norms of "ladylike" behavior. In other words, these women "killed like men."

3. Because women commit such a small fraction of the kinds of murders that qualify for the death penalty, "gender-neutral" rather than "gender-based" factors account for women's experiences with capital punishment. Current law holds that killing strangers for private gain is more heinous than killing inmates in anger. Men are more likely to kill for gain; women are more likely to kill inmates.

Dana then began to fill in this structure with evidence, for instance, listing these subtopics under the first answer:

- Cite current number of men versus women on death row.
- Brief historical view of how infrequently women are executed compared with men.
- Give a couple of examples showing that women can be as heinous as men when murdering yet do not receive the death penalty.
- The "femininity loophole," or why women can't be executed: "She had PMS," "She was emotionally overwrought," "She was dominated or abused by a man," "She's a mother," "She is not a threat."
- Cite petition from male San Quentin inmates pleading to spare the life of a condemned female or to be killed in her place.
- Cite statistics indicating reversal or commutation of death sentences for women who have effectively been remolded into traditional womanhood during prison: sewing, religion, etc.

At this point, Dana was able to reorder points or subdivide them further, or leave them and move on to developing the second and third answers into a complete outline.

A SAMPLE STUDENT OUTLINE

Here is Tanaya Burnham's complete outline for a paper on multiracial identity in the United States. It answers the question "How do multiracial individuals develop a positive self-identity when societies, as well as members of their own racial groups, often reject them?"

I. Introduction: In the United States people tend to be classified by their race, but what about those whose parentage is not monoracial?
II. Laws that forbade interracial marriage
   A. History of antimiscegenation laws
   B. Consequences of antimiscegenation laws
III. Interracial families and multiracial identity
   A. Who is likely to marry outside their race?
   B. Implications of multiracial identity
      1. Group rejection
      2. Multiracial identity
IV. The multiracial baby boom
   A. The 2010 U. S. Census
V. Conclusion

A computer tip.
Most word-processing programs, such as Microsoft Word, have outlining capabilities. If your word processor has this outlining function, learn how to use it. You may want to use it later to begin drafting your paper by inserting material. Open two files so you can access and move information between two corresponding windows: (1) your notes and/or outline and (2) your developing draft of the paper. Most writers move back and forth between their outline and rough draft as work on one modifies the other. Alternatively, most word-processing programs allow you to insert text beneath each outline item, where you can write the body of your paper, then hide the outline.

WRITING A DRAFT

Once you have gathered your ideas, you are ready to write the first draft. As previously discussed, the thought of producing a complete paper in one sitting can induce writing anxiety and procrastination. Don't feel that you need to write the entire paper at once. Some people find it helpful to make a schedule of writing, with writing sessions at different times.

If you have created an outline or even a string of boxes with your main points, choose one that is clearest and begin writing your draft. Remember, you may change it later.

If you still feel stuck, follow the surprising advice expert rhetorician Ross Winterowd gave to a struggling graduate student: "lower your standards." Don't wait for the perfect opening line, thesis, or argument. Imagine that you are speaking to a friend. What would you say if you didn't have to find exactly the right words? You might start writing something like the following: "What I'd like to say is . . ." Keep going. You can revise later.

Experiment with imitating the form and language of published texts and sample student papers in sociology. This imitation is not the same as plagiarism to be discussed in Chapter 5 because you are not copying other writers' ideas or specific sentences. Instead, carefully observe what types of introductions and conclusions are typical, how writers structure paragraphs, the kinds of words they use to add examples or make transitions, and other details of organization and style. Writing for academic audiences often employs typical formats or templates to structure arguments. Imitating such a template can help you get started on your own writing. For an example, read a student's revised paragraph on page 9. The student uses conventional language but also effectively lays out what has been learned from sources and what the argument will be. Notice the key phrases: *according to . . . ; for example . . . ; however . . . ; two paradigms predominate . . . ; despite conflicting explanations, all agree . . . ; I therefore. . . .* Like a map, a model can help you find ways to navigate through your writing.

If necessary, make time to return to your original research articles, books, or other data. Avoid adding fluff to fulfill a particular word or page requirement. Look again at the argument each source makes and check that you're explaining it fully. Add additional sources if you need more support for your ideas.

There is no magic order for sentences in a paragraph. The main idea may be first, last, or in between. A lot depends on how the previous paragraph ended. All sentences in a paragraph should be about the same idea and you should be able to write a short sentence summarizing each paragraph.

This is not the time to polish those sentences—move on to the next point. You can make the connections and smooth things out later.

Notice in the paragraph below, how Tanaya builds two paragraphs around one main point from her outline. Tanaya begins with the heading, "Group rejection," and makes this general point, "Qualitative research on biracial and multiracial individuals showed that these individuals often experienced more discrimination by their own racial groups than by groups outside their racial heritage." She then develops two paragraphs for this point: one paragraph is about the main idea of discrimination experienced by children within their own families and the other is about the main idea of discrimination of such children by members of their own racial groups.

SAMPLE STUDENT PARAGRAPHS

Multiracial children can experience prejudice within their own families as well. The birth of children to an interracial couple experiencing tensions within their extended family could either bring the family together, proving blood ties are stronger than racial barriers, or could even tear the family further apart (Root 2001). Some grandparents have been known to disown their own children and the interracial family altogether, leaving the multiracial children feeling a sense of abandonment from their extended families (Root 2001). Tensions between one side of the family and a parent can cause the multiracial child to have questions of loyalty (Root 2001). Multiracial children can also feel abandoned by their own parents as well, such as when a parent shows preference for monoracial siblings (Brown 2001).

Multiracial individuals often experience more discrimination by their own racial groups than by groups outside their racial heritage (Stephen and Stephan 1991; Root 2001). Multiracial children were taunted with racial terms like "Oreo," "mutt," "wannabe," etc., from children of their own race (Tizard and Phoenix 2002). Young adults of Korean and white ancestry recount how they were excluded by the white community for being Asian and excluded by the Korean community for not being Korean enough (Standen 1996). They were also criticized for not knowing how to speak Korean fluently or for being too Americanized (Standen 1996). Multiracial individuals are subjected to a higher standard of cultural competence compared with monoracial children of the same immigrant generation (Standen 1996). I, too, have a similar experience because even though all of my American-born full Korean cousins and I are not fluent in the Korean language, my fellow biracial cousins and I are more criticized by my family for our inability to converse in Korean. Multiracial individuals also run the risk of being considered cultural traitors. Especially if one parent is white, there seems to be a fear by the minority race that their culture will be left behind and the multiracial children will choose to perpetuate the dominant culture over their

A computer tip.
If you find yourself getting stuck trying to illustrate a point, explain an illustration, or complete a thought, embed a symbol system such as XXX that you can use later to easily locate those places with the "Find" command in Microsoft Word.

ethnic one (Root 2001). This fear also brings concern about who the multiracial child will marry and how they will rear their children. Some multiracial children from Asian families were encouraged to marry someone of their same Asian ethnicity (Winters and DeBose 2003).

GETTING FEEDBACK AND REVISING

Once you have written a draft of your paper, your next step is to revise it. Revising can greatly improve the logic and structure of your argument (these two features are discussed in Chapter 2). Revising includes inserting new ideas and deleting or modifying old ones, rewriting sentences or paragraphs to improve clarity or logic, moving sentences or paragraphs around to strengthen organization, and adding transitions to enhance the flow of your writing and accentuate the relationships among your ideas. For example, examine the two paragraphs above: one paragraph is about discrimination within families, and one is about discrimination from one's own racial group. Do you think any of the sentences in the second paragraph would be more appropriate in the first paragraph and should be moved up? This is the kind of question to ask yourself at this stage. Setting your draft aside for a few days between revisions helps you more clearly see its strengths and weaknesses, and possibilities for revision.

When you are satisfied with the logical order of your paragraphs and with the order and adequacy of the sentences in each paragraph, you need to look carefully at each sentence. At this stage, most writers rely on three revision techniques: *eliminating wordiness, adding details and examples,* and *adding transitional expressions.* Following is a sample paragraph from a student's draft proposal for a paper on stress management. The paragraphs are in the proper order in the paper and the sentences come in the right order in the paragraph, but the writing is not graceful. This paragraph is grammatically correct but could be improved. Notice how the student has applied these three revision techniques to improve the paragraph.

Original draft paragraph:

From the readings I did for the course on stress, I have found that there have been many studies done to try to find the single most common cause of stress. Some stress scholars believe it is the major life changes that provoke stress. Others believe that it is the everyday hassles and annoyances of life which bring about stress. Despite the conflicting viewpoints in the causality of stress, all scholars agree that when stressful stimuli can be recognized and regulated early there seem to be less damaging effects on the body. At this point I have a confident feeling that I will be able to locate good, current information on the questions of stress management, which I intend to research. (121 words)

1. **Eliminate Wordiness.** The following can lead to wordiness in writing:
   - Redundant pairs ("everyday hassles and annoyances")
   - Inflated phrases ("At this point")
   - Intensifiers ("single most common")
   - Action in a noun rather than a verb ("a confident feeling")
   - Passive voice ("be recognized and regulated")
   - Expletives ("it is")

Paragraph revised to eliminate wordiness:

According to my readings about stress, many studies have tried to find its most common cause. According to some scholars, major life changes provoke stress; for others, everyday annoyances cause it. Despite conflicting explanations, all agree that early recognition and regulation lessen bodily damage. I feel confident now that I can locate good, relevant information on stress management. (58 words)

2. **Add Details and Examples.** Details answer the journalistic questions "Who?" "What" "Where" "When?" "Why?" and "How?" Examples can be illustrations you create or evidence you cite.

Paragraph revised to add details and examples:

According to my readings about stress, many studies have tried to find its most common cause. *Loss and Trauma: General and Close Relationship Perspective*s (2000) includes 24 chapters by different social scientists. According to some scholars, major life changes provoke stress; others argue that everyday annoyances cause it. Two paradigms predominate: the "stress model," especially in medical sociology and psychology, and the "normative development" model, especially in life-span development research. Despite conflicting explanations, all agree that early recognition and regulation lessen bodily damage. I feel confident now that I can locate good, relevant information on stress management. (98 words)

3. **Add Transitional Expressions.** Transitional words function like traffic signals, directing the reader from one sentence to the next by identifying the logical relationship between these sentences.
   - **To show addition:** *again, also, and, and then, besides, equally important, further, furthermore, moreover, next, similarly, too, what's more*
   - **To show time:** *after, afterward, as, at length, at once, at the same time, by, earlier, eventually, finally, first, formerly, gradually, immediately, later, next, once, previously, second, soon, then, thereafter, while*
   - **To make the reader stop and compare:** *after all, although, at the same time, but, conversely, for all that, however, in contrast, in the meantime, meanwhile, nevertheless, nonetheless, notwithstanding, on the contrary, on the other hand, still, whereas, yet*

- **To give examples:** *as an illustration, for example, for instance, in other words, to demonstrate, to illustrate*
- **To emphasize:** *as a matter of fact, clearly, in any case, in any event, in fact, indeed, more important, obviously, of course, that is*
- **To repeat:** *as I have said (demonstrated, argued, noted), in brief, in other words, in short*
- **To draw a conclusion:** *accordingly, as a result, at last, consequently, hence, in brief, in conclusion, in sum, on the whole, so, therefore, thus, to conclude*

Paragraph revised to add transitional expressions:

According to my readings about stress, many studies have tried to find its most common cause. For example, *Loss and Trauma: General and Close Relationship Perspectives* (2000) includes 24 chapters by different social scientists. According to some scholars, major life changes provoke stress; however, others argue that everyday annoyances cause it. Two paradigms predominate: first, the "stress model," especially in medical sociology and psychology, and, second, the "normative development" model, especially in life-span development research. Despite conflicting explanations, all agree that early recognition and regulation lessen bodily damage. I therefore feel confident now that I can locate good, relevant information on stress management. (104 words)

Note this final, revised paragraph still includes fewer words than the original draft. However, every word adds meaning. The result is clear, concise, logical writing.

When revising, think carefully about your paper's key concepts and terms. Define them as you introduce them (usually in the opening paragraphs) and use them accurately throughout the paper. Be especially cautious when using terms originated by sociologists that have become part of everyday language and yet retain special sociological meaning (for example, "stereotype," "status," "self-fulfilling prophecy"). General dictionaries are written to reflect the ordinary usage of words, which are often different from sociological definitions. Thus you should avoid using dictionaries to define sociological concepts. If you are unsure, we recommend that you consult one of the following specialized dictionaries in the reference section of your college library: *A New Dictionary of the Social Sciences, A Modern Dictionary of Sociology,* or *Dictionary of Modern Sociology.* Several such dictionaries are now online. It's often helpful to write out sociological definitions of your central terms on scratch paper—in language you can understand—in order to foster clear and accurate use of them as you revise. When dealing with words that do not have special sociological meaning, a good dictionary and a thesaurus can help you both to locate the most precise word that expresses what you want to say and to find synonyms for varying your word choice.

An Internet tip.
References such as dictionary.com and thesaurus.reference.com can be helpful in finding the ordinary definition of words. However, the online Dictionary of the Social Sciences (http://sociology.socialscience-dictionary.com/Sociology-Dictionary/) is preferable for sociological terms.

Language for referring to social groups. The revising stage is also the time to troubleshoot your draft for biased or sexist language. The appropriate language to refer to people in general—men vs. women and various racial or ethnic groups—has changed dramatically over the last several decades. The issue of gendered language has been especially emphasized, not because gender inequality is any more important than other bases of inequality, but because there was a time when people were taught gendered language was proper grammar, that "he" and "him" were the correct way to refer to both men and women. Many writers were insensitive to the negative connotations of words they used to describe racial, ethnic, and sexual minorities. Norms and practices have changed, so that terms for all people are gender neutral and more respectful toward minority groups. At this point you need to check to see if you inadvertently used sexist or biased language. Although most writers prefer to use nonsexist language, repeating "he or she" every time a singular pronoun is required can sound awkward and repetitive. The *ASA Style Guide* makes several suggestions for avoiding sexist language: whenever possible use a gender neutral term for labels (*child* instead of *boy* or *girl*, *firefighter* instead of *fireman*, *chair* instead of *chairman*). Use a plural pronoun such as *people* or *they*. Replace gendered pronouns with an article (change *his* to *the*). Delete pronouns altogether (*ASA Style Guide*, 2010: 4–5). If you are unsure, check with your instructor to see how she or he prefers writing be made gender neutral.

This is also the time to check how all social groups are referenced. Sound sociological writing should refer to minority groups, religious groups, sub-cultural groups, and groups with nontypical physical characteristics with terms that show respect and accuracy. As sociologists we know language can contain stereotypes and carry consequences for members of groups. Further clarification can be found in the *ASA Style Guide* (2010:4-5), the *Chicago Manual of Style* (2003: 157, 233), or the American Psychological Association Style Web site (http://apastyle.org/manual/supplement/index.aspx).

Internet Tip:

The Writing Center at the University of North Carolina–Chapel Hill has a useful guide for using gender-neutral language: http://writingcenter.unc.edu/resources/handouts-demos/citation/gender-sensitive-language.

ACADEMIC WRITING STYLES

The craft of writing requires as much attention to how ideas are expressed as to content. "Style" refers to *how* the author expresses ideas. "Style" has two main meanings. First, it can refer to the impression your writing creates about you. Your writing can make you sound friendly and informal, pompous, careless and sloppy, emotionally involved, or scientifically detached. We all have different writing styles for different occasions. Second, "style" can also refer to professional standards about the expected format for displaying your paper on the page and for identifying and citing the information you borrow from sources.

Just as people dress differently, speak differently, and behave differently in different social situations, writers choose different words and sentence structures depending on the writing situation and their readers. Therefore, writers do not have only one style, and no one style is better than another. You will address a classmate in a personal Instant Message differently from the way you write when you e-mail a question to your instructor. One will likely be more informal. Assigned papers will be more formal. Good writers learn to vary their linguistic wardrobe to the occasion and adjust their styles to their readers.

One problem with academic style in assigned papers is trying to compensate for uncertainty with verbal bravado—using big words and complex sentence structures to sound intelligent. Sociologists have been frequently criticized for using too much jargon and for writing in a convoluted style that is difficult to comprehend. Some students try to copy that style, thinking it will make their writing seem "academic." That defeats the purpose of writing, which is to communicate. The best writing is usually easy to read and understand. The intelligence is in the ideas, not the vocabulary. Students often think if they sound intelligent they will earn a better grade than if they write intelligently. Occasionally an instructor will give a higher grade to papers with fancy words, but most focus on the ideas.

Remember these tips:

+ Don't use a big word when a small one will do.
+ Use contractions (for example, "it's," "don't," "you're") as you draft your paper if they feel more natural to you than writing the words out ("it is," "do not," "you are"). Before you revise your final draft, however, ask if your instructor objects. If you have waited until the last minute and do not know your instructor's preference—which may vary according to the type of assignment—then play it safe and avoid contractions (for example, they are not appropriate for the journal format).
+ Use specialized sociological terms only to be precise about the concept you are discussing.
+ Each sentence should include only one thought or idea.
+ Try to use active rather than passive verbs wherever possible to ensure that both writer and reader know *who* is "doing the doing." Too much use of the passive voice can create ambiguity about the social processes under discussion.
+ Avoid using too many prepositional phrases, which can fill sentences with modifiers of modifiers and make them difficult to read.
+ Use adverbs and adjectives sparingly. Some people think that good writing means filling your text with flowery adverbs and adjectives. Make sure that the modifiers you use add meaning and not just filler to your text.
+ Remember that reading your paper should be a pleasure, not a chore.

What your writing looks like on the page. It is a good idea to locate a manual of style—which presents standards and examples of grammar, punctuation, usage, and typography—to answer specific questions that may arise during the writing process. If your paper includes tables and graphs, choose a manual

"Making the simple complicated is commonplace; making the complicated simple, awesomely simple, that's creativity."

Charles Mingus

that also provides guidelines on how information should be arranged and labeled. (The style manuals we recommend below include such guidelines and are available in many libraries and online.) Early in the quarter/semester, before the almost inevitable end-of-the-term crunch, ask your instructor to recommend a manual; you can put it aside until you need it. If your instructor doesn't have a preference, you may choose the inexpensive, but useful and brief (128 pages) paperback *ASA Style Guide* (2010) available from the American Sociological Association or from the ASA Online Bookstore at http://www. e-noah.net/asa/asashoponlineservice/. *The Chicago Manual of Style* is long and comprehensive; it is available both in print and online (for a subscription fee) <http://www.chicagomanualofstyle.org/home.html>; however, you can get a one-time only 30-day free trial. If you only need help with citations, you can use the *Chicago-Style Citation Quick Guide* at http://www.chicagomanualof-style.org/tools_citationguide.html for free. We also suggest the inexpensive, popular paperback edition of Kate L. Turabian's *A Manual for Writers of Term Papers, Dissertations, and Theses*, which recommends many of the same style standards suggested by *The Chicago Manual of Style*. If anxiety about standards and rules impedes your writing, don't think about a manual until you have generated at least one draft.

SUMMING UP

Writing is a *process*. There are many stages, involving different skills, different kinds of thinking, and different levels of concentration. A student should not expect to sit down and instantly create a good paper any more than instructors just sit down and write a lecture or a research article. Some students feel more comfortable and more skilled at some parts of the process than others. Nearly everyone—including their professors—feels insecure about some parts of the process. Further, there is no single correct *process* for writing sociology papers. Each step will be done differently by different writers: some like to read about a topic before generating a question, some begin with the question. Some construct an outline and then fill in the text; others write a draft and cut and paste so they can prepare an outline. Some like to craft a sentence as they write, while others get everything on paper and repeatedly revise. The fundamental principle is that conforming to any particular process is less important than doing what works for each author. Of course, that does not mean "anything goes." Quality still matters. The goal of the writer is to find what process works best and to consistently and self-consciously hone the craftsmanship, so the desired level of quality is achieved.

2

Working with Sources

The accumulation of knowledge is a group activity. Scholars build on and respond to one another's data (concepts, insights, theories, and statistics) that circulate through conference papers, articles, and books. When you write your paper, you are engaging in this process. You can better answer a sociological question by knowing how others have answered it. Even if you are not assigned to read beyond your textbook, you will want to learn more about the topic. You will write a better paper if you know more about the subject. Chapter 4, "Collecting and Evaluating Sources," offers suggestions on finding appropriate sources. Most students can effectively search topics online and find reliable and sociologically sound information. But what do you do when you find the material? Chapter 5, "Citing Sources and Preparing Bibliographies," discusses how to use the sources you have found to successfully write a paper. Plagiarism and attribution will be addressed and a specialty assignment sometimes found in sociological papers—the annotated bibliography—will also be introduced.

Collecting and Evaluating Sources

Research is formalized curiosity. It is poking and prying with a purpose.

ZORA NEALE HURSTON

While it may be fun to learn about a topic, the process of digging up sources, wading through masses of information, and organizing what you have read can be daunting. The Information Age presents us with mountains of data. Students often feel overwhelmed by so much information. This chapter attempts to make the challenge of finding, evaluating, and keeping track of library and electronic sources more manageable.

Several strategies and techniques can help you determine where to start, how to search for potential sources with keywords, how to evaluate the quality of potential sources, and how to keep track of those sources. We will present these techniques sequentially, but the research process is messy. Expect to circle back and search for additional sources.

BEFORE YOU START: CHOOSING A TOPIC

You often start a library research project with little information about your topic. How then do you begin developing a good question for your paper to focus on?

First, select a general subject area that is interesting and relevant to your course. One way to find a topic is by skimming your syllabus and course readings. Review the entire syllabus because a topic that will be discussed later in the course might be the basis for a good research question. Your instructor can help at this stage by letting you know if your research question is on target.

Next, construct provisional questions. For example, if you want to study the feminist movement in the United States, ask yourself why this topic interests you. Your personal interest in a subject will motivate and guide you during the research and writing process. Decide which aspect of the subject you will investigate. In the case of feminism you may want to focus your research on wage differences ("Are women's wages lower than men's?"), on power differences ("What determines the relative power of men and women inside families?"), or on ways people learn to fill the gender roles expected of them ("How are males and females socialized to enact sex-role stereotypes in their daily lives?").

Remember to maintain a sociological perspective. The examples given in the previous paragraph are sociologically relevant because they highlight differences between groups of people (men and women) and because they focus on patterned relationships in the social world. A review of Chapter 1 will help stimulate the sociological imagination you need to ask a good question.

DETERMINING YOUR FIRST SOURCE(S)

"Knowledge is of two kinds. We know a subject ourselves, or we know where we can find information upon it."

Samuel Johnson

Quality, not quantity, is what counts in collecting research sources. Finding *enough* sources for your topic is usually easy; finding the *right* sources can be challenging. Should you start with a newspaper, a professional journal or magazine article, a general or specialized encyclopedia article, a government Web site, or a book? If you have a destination in mind, you are more likely to have a successful research journey. Planning your initial search for sources involves several factors: How recent is the information that you need? How much do you know about the topic? and What type of research paper have you been assigned?

Different sources contain information from authors with varying degrees of professional expertise. Here is an example of what kinds of information the student researching the topic of the single-parent family would find in various sources:

Newspaper: immediately newsworthy current events and local coverage; for example, City Council budget provisions for day care or stories about single parents on welfare. Most newspapers now have Web sites, though many charge for displaying items in their archives.

Magazine: recent current affairs and enduring popular topics; for example, a cover story on the state of marriage in the United States or a profile ranking Fortune 500 companies with the best day care programs. While most magazines have Web sites, many do not post the full content of their paper editions.

Journal: scholarly research results of specialists' studies conducted in the last few years; for example, case studies of economic and educational prospects of children growing up in single-parent homes. Most scholarly journals have electronic editions, though they may need to be accessed through a university computer or they may require your Web browser have a university proxy. Your librarian or campus computing service can help you set that up. In general, journals that have been "peer-reviewed" are of higher quality than those that have not. "Peer review" means that before publishing, articles are reviewed by academic experts to ensure that the methods are reliable and that the scholarly quality is acceptable.

These journals will state that they are peer-reviewed in each issue and on their Web sites.

Book: in-depth coverage of a topic or collections of scholarly articles compiled over the last few years; for example, a history of family structure in the United States or a long-term study of single-parent families in Canada.

Encyclopedia: the big picture of what is known about a topic; for example, ways in which parents influence the social development of children or the forms of family organization in different cultures. There are general encyclopedias online, such as Wikipedia, but they should be used cautiously and cannot substitute for more serious academic scholarship.

World Wide Web (Internet): spans the range above; for example, information obtained from instantaneous chat room discussions for single parents to archived statistical government information from the U. S. Department of Health and Human Services. There are increasing amounts of reliable and unreliable information and opinions on the Web in the form of blogs, RSS feeds, and other sources.

These sources represent information processed over time. Consider then which information you will need most, especially at the beginning of your search. For example, a student researching the legalization of same-sex marriage would need to rely on newspapers, magazines, and the Internet to read about recent developments in particular states where legislatures have been considering new laws; whereas a student investigating the disappearance of the gift economy in South Pacific societies would consult books and scholarly journal articles. Also consider how much you know about your topic. You may need to begin with an overview in a general or specialized encyclopedia, either online or in print. If you have been studying the topic in class and are able to understand the details, you may prefer beginning with a recent professional journal article. When selecting an information source, remember that some book publishers and authors are more reliable than others. For example, most students would know tabloid magazines are not appropriate for college research papers unless tabloids were the topic being researched. Additionally, authors can be dishonest, misinformed, or mistaken, leaving readers to rely on journal and book editors to select reliable writing. We can identify a few guidelines for choosing reliable sources:

+ Academic journals are more reliable than popular magazines. Some academic journals, such as *American Sociological Review*, may be difficult for undergraduates to read, especially the articles with complex statistics. But you can get the gist of such articles and consult the bibliographic references at the ends of the articles. Although popular magazines should not be excluded altogether, be cautious of their contents.

+ University presses (such as Cambridge University Press or Harvard University Press) are less likely to print poorly researched books than are commercial presses. For commercially published books, those written by academics are usually more reliable than those written by journalists.

✦ Articles and books that carefully cite their sources of information are more reliable than those that don't. While some students find a heavily footnoted article or book daunting, these references provide the reader with the means to verify the author's assertions.

FINDING SOURCES ON THE WEB

"Being a good writer is 3% talent, 97% not being distracted by the Internet."

Anonymous

One of the principles students learn in college is that all knowledge is not created equal: the print and electronic information available through a library is usually trustworthy, whereas information available through the Internet can be unreliable. It may appear authoritative, but further scrutiny reveals it to be incomplete, commercially or otherwise biased, out of date, or wrong. While Internet information may be questionable, it may include links to valuable data. How can you determine the value of a potential research source? What specific features of a source reveal its worth and allow you to evaluate its reliability?

USING GENERAL INTERNET SEARCH ENGINES

While many students begin a search with general search engines such as *Google, Yahoo!*, or *Bing*, unless specifically looking for journalistic articles, we recommend trying more scholarly and specialized resources such as *Google Scholar*, first. As emphasized above, the general search engines have no quality controls.

If you search on a general search engine such as *Google*, you will find a variety of links from reliable scholarly sources to highly partisan activists to tabloid journalism. If you are interested in studying *about* partisan activists or tabloid journalism, those sites will be useful. But if you are interested in using the sources for the information they deliver, you need to apply the criteria discussed below.

CRITERIA FOR ASSESSING WEB PAGES

Filtering out useless information on the Internet is essential. We recommend applying the following five criteria for assessing Web pages:

1. Credibility of Local Origin. Where does the information come from? Before you link to a WWW data source, check its electronic address, known as its uniform resource locator (URL). If the address includes the abbreviation *edu* or *gov* (which identifies its association with an educational institution or government agency), you may find more reliable information than if the URL has the abbreviation *org* (organization) or *com* (commercial). Other less common abbreviations, such as *net*, also exist. On some search engines, such as *Google*, you can specify the domain by adding "site:edu" or "site:gov" (without the quotation marks) after your initial keyword. For example, if you were looking for government Web sites with information about single parents, you could search "single parent* site:gov" (without quotation marks).

Examples

\<http://www.census.gov/\>	(the U. S. Census Bureau)
\<http://www.soc.qc.edu/\>	(the Sociology Department at Queens College, CUNY)
\<http://www.aclu-sc.org/\>	(American Civil Liberties Union of Southern California)
\<http://singleparentsnetwork.com/\>	(A resource site for single parents)

We are *not* suggesting that organizational or commercial Web sites are automatically inferior. The American Civil Liberties Union of Southern California, for instance, provides texts of legislation, starting with the Bill of Rights, and updates about the progress of pending legislative initiatives from the organization's point of view. Similarly, Single Parent Central offers a broad variety of books and articles from government sources about single parenting, though most are written for single parents rather than for scholarly studies. It also includes facts about single-parent families.

2. Accountability. Is there an author or sponsor identified on the Web page with an e-mail link? Is there a link on the page back to its "home"? Useful sources provide this information about their data.

3. Timeliness. When was the Web page last updated? Is the information still accurate? Online information quickly becomes obsolete.

4. Scope and Coverage. Does the information on the Web page seem well researched? Are useful links embedded in the page? How does the online information compare with what you have found on paper? Are the graphics worth the download time?

5. Reputation. Is the Web site sponsored by or linked to a reputable organization? Ask your instructor, teaching assistant, or librarian about unconfirmed sources.

WIKIPEDIA

The online encyclopedia Wikipedia \<http://en.wikipedia.org/wiki/Main_Page\> is one of the most impressive achievements of our virtual society. Thousands of volunteers gather information on every conceivable topic and correct mistakes to amass the greatest volume of knowledge ever gathered. Wikipedia's greatest strength, however, is also its greatest weakness: anyone can contribute information. These sometimes unverified contributions highlight the important issue of reliability. Because Wikipedia also allows other readers to correct mistakes, controversial issues and obscure topics are vulnerable to distorted information. But with its vast amount of information and its ease of use, students can be inclined to overuse Wikipedia. Many teachers have become concerned with this dependence and prohibit its use in papers. Wikipedia proves most beneficial in the research process when limited to use as a starting point for learning basic information about a topic. It should be used as a source to build a foundation for further exploration; however, users are advised to read and evaluate the information carefully.

As with other Internet sources, searching for specific topics or facts in Wikipedia can be difficult if the terminology used in your search differs from terminology commonly used by sociologists. For example, a general *Google* search for "women executed in the United States" returned over 12 million hits, but the third and fourth links, which indicate the rate at which users follow the links, were to Wikipedia hits including "List of females executed in the United States." To learn the relative number of men and women executed, you would have to follow the link to "Capital punishment in the United States," which would show that only 0.9% of those executed in the United States since 1976 have been women.

INTERNET DATA SOURCES

The Internet can also be an excellent source of data. *Google* can identify specialized U. S. Government Web sites <http://www.google.com/unclesam> that provide current government information, while the U. S. Census Bureau Web site <http://www.census.gov> provides demographic data about various population issues in graphic and tabular formats such as maps and statistics. The Census site also provides downloadable software for census and survey processing, and access to Census Bureau online roundtables, which are forums where the public can read and post follow-up comments. Other links that provide access to downloadable data but require some knowledge of quantitative techniques include:

General Social Survey (GSS) The GSS contains a standard 'core' of demographic, behavioral, and attitudinal questions, plus topics of special interest. Many of the core questions have remained unchanged since 1972 to facilitate time-trend studies as well as replication of earlier findings. For an introduction to the data set and how to use it, see their Web site. <http://www.norc.org/GSS+Website>

FEDSTATS This is a portal to 70 federal, state, and local government agencies that collect and report statistics. <http://www.fedstats.gov/>

The Gallup Poll Results of public opinion polls on a broad variety of topics. <http://www.galluppoll.com/>

WHERE TO FIND SPECIFIC INFORMATION

SPECIALIZED DICTIONARIES AND ENCYCLOPEDIAS

These references explain key terms and concepts, and provide background information about key historical figures. Several sociological dictionaries can be accessed at <http://www.yourdictionary.com/dictionary-articles/sociology-dictionary.html>. The advantage of beginning with specialized dictionaries or encyclopedias is they can provide a quick overview of a subject; however, the disadvantage is that sources are not usually current.

ONLINE LIBRARY CATALOG

The main Web site of libraries will have a search facility or an easy link to a search page for its books and journals. Finding information by searching the catalog by author and title is straightforward, but the organization of subject headings may follow a logic that differs from how you think about your topic. If you look for books by subject and don't find any information, it may be because the subject you are looking for is not an official subject category. For example, if your paper is on the implications of regulating handguns, your search under the subject "Handguns" or "Handgun Control," may not find anything. "Handguns" and "Handgun Control" are not official topics in subject categorization systems; you must consult a special reference book to find official topics called "subject headings." This reference book, called *The Library of Congress Subject Headings*, is usually found at the reference desk. When you look up "Handguns" in *The Library of Congress Subject Headings*, you will find this instruction: "See Pistols;" if you look up "Handgun Control" in *The Library of Congress Subject Headings*, you will find "See Gun Control." You will also learn "Works on legal aspects of gun control are entered under 'Firearms—Law and legislation.'" Finding books by subject can require this detective work to find the right subject heading.

The Library of Congress Subject Headings is now available online at http://id.loc.gov/authorities/subjects.html.

JOURNALS OFTEN USED BY SOCIOLOGISTS

Scholars, apprentice scholars, and undergraduates rely on journal articles and books to keep up with new research and professional opinions.

While the following list of sociology periodicals in Table 4–1 is not exhaustive, it will give you a sense of the discipline's ongoing research. Additionally, it might trigger ideas about topics for future papers. Although the articles in these journals are intended primarily for a scholarly audience rather than the general public, you will find many articles easily accessible. For more references to specialized journals and governmental sources, ask your reference librarian. Many of the Web sites listed are accessible only from a university computer or one that has a university proxy in the browser software. The descriptions of each journal are taken from the journals themselves.

If you know something about the topic, consider beginning with a review article published in the *Annual Review of Sociology*. These articles are written by experts in various sociological specialties on recent developments in their fields. Each article includes an extensive bibliography on the topic, making the articles valuable as both a summary of recent scholarship and as a source for finding books and articles on your topic. It can be found in paper versions in college libraries or online at http://www.annualreviews.org/loi/soc; however, like many sources, the Web site is restricted, requiring access through your library or with a college proxy.

TABLE 4-1

American Journal of Sociology Published by the *University of Chicago Press*, this influential journal includes theoretical and research articles, book reviews, and commentaries on articles published previously. <http://www.press.uchicago.edu/ucp/journals/journal/ajs.html>

American Sociological Review Published by the *American Sociological Association (ASA)*, this review covers diverse areas of sociology, often with a statistical and empirical orientation. <http://www.asanet.org/journals/asr/>

City and Community Published by the *ASA Section on Community and Urban Sociology*, this journal encompasses theoretical and empirical articles about communities and places, both urban and rural. <http://www.blackwellpublishing.com/journal.asp?ref=1535-6841&site=1>

Contemporary Sociology Published by the *ASA*, its special feature is to review books, journals, articles, and films that cover a wide range of areas, such as historical and comparative sociology, social psychology, gender, education, and stratification. The review essays are especially useful for learning about new publications and sociologists' evaluations of them. <http://csx.sagepub.com/>

Contexts This nontechnical magazine published by the *ASA* covers timely sociological ideas and research about society and social behavior. <http://contexts.org/>

Criminology This interdisciplinary journal emphasizes research in the social and behavioral sciences about crime and deviant behavior, and presents articles on the theoretical and historical components of crime, law, and criminal justice. <http://www.wiley.com/bw/journal.asp?ref=0011-1384>

Demography This interdisciplinary journal, published by the *Population Association of America*, includes research studies on developing countries as well as developed countries. <http://muse.jhu.edu/journals/dem/>

Gender and Society This interdisciplinary journal is sponsored by *Sociologists for Women in Society*. It aims to advance the study of gender, as well as racial, ethnic, cultural, and national diversity. <http://gas.sagepub.com/>

International Migration Review (IMR) This journal is an interdisciplinary journal created to encourage and facilitate the study of all aspects of sociodemographic, historical, economic, political, legislative and international migration. It is internationally regarded as the principal journal in the field facilitating study of international migration, ethnic group relations, and refugee movements. Through an interdisciplinary approach and from an international perspective, *IMR* provides the single most comprehensive forum devoted exclusively to the analysis and review of international population movements. <http://www.wiley.com/bw/journal.asp?ref=0197-9183>

Journal for the Scientific Study of Religion This multidisciplinary journal covers articles, research notes, and book reviews on the social-scientific study of religion. Published articles are representative of the best current theoretical and methodological treatments of religion. Substantive areas include both micro-level and macro-level analyses of religious organizations, institutions, and social change. While many articles published in the journal are sociological, the journal also publishes the work of psychologists, political scientists, anthropologists, and economists. <http://onlinelibrary.wiley.com/journal/10.1111/%28ISSN%291468-5906>

Journal of Aging Studies This publication highlights innovative research approaches, critiques of existing theory, and empirical work related to age and aging. <http://www.elsevier.com/wps/find/journaldescription.cws_home/620198/description#description>

Journal of Contemporary Ethnography This journal presents ethnographic studies based on qualitative interviewing and participant observation. <http://jce.sagepub.com/>

Journal of Gerontology: Social Sciences The social science edition of this journal is published by the *Gerontological Society of America*. This interdisciplinary journal seeks to promote the scientific study of aging and the life course. <http://psychsocgerontology.oxfordjournals.org/>

Journal of Health and Social Behavior Published by the *ASA*, this journal uses a sociological perspective in understanding health-related issues; for example, organizational aspects of hospitals or class characteristics of sufferers from various illnesses. <http://hsb.sagepub.com/>

Journal of Marriage and the Family Published by the *National Council on Family Relations*, this journal covers such diverse research areas as family planning, family structure, theories of the family, and cross-cultural studies on fertility. Each issue also features a book review section. <http://onlinelibrary.wiley.com/journal/10.1111/%28ISSN%291741-3737>

Journal of Personality and Social Psychology Published by the *American Psychological Association (APA)*, this journal is divided into sections on attitudes and social cognition, interpersonal relations and group processes, and personality processes and individual differences. <http://www.apa.org/journals/psp/>

Poetics This interdisciplinary journal covers theoretical and empirical research on culture, the media, and the arts. <http://www.journals.elsevier.com/poetics>

Politics and Society This journal presents articles that raise questions about the way the world is organized politically, economically, and socially. <http://pas.sagepub.com/>

Population Studies The journal's coverage of this field is comprehensive: applications in developed and developing countries; historical and contemporary studies; quantitative and qualitative studies; analytical essays and reviews. The subjects of papers range from classical concerns, such as the determinants and consequences of population change, to such topics as family demography and evolutionary and genetic influences on demographic behavior. Often the journal's papers have had the effect of extending the boundaries of its field. <http://www2.lse.ac.uk/socialPolicy/researchcentresandgroups/PIC/populationStudies/aims.aspx>

Qualitative Sociology This journal publishes research based on qualitative research methods, such as interviewing, participant observation, ethnography, historical analysis, and content analysis. <http://www.springer.com/social+sciences/journal/11133>

Ethnic and Racial Studies This is the leading journal for the analysis of these issues throughout the world. The journal provides an interdisciplinary academic forum for the presentation of research and theoretical analysis, drawing on sociology, social policy, anthropology, political science, economics, geography, international relations, history, social psychology, and cultural studies. <http://www.tandfonline.com/toc/rers20/current>

Rural Sociology This journal publishes new approaches to emerging issues, recurring questions and material, and policy relevant discussions of changes in local and global systems affecting rural people and places. <http://www.wiley.com/WileyCDA/WileyTitle/productCd-RUSO.html>

Sex Roles: A Journal of Research This journal presents empirical and theoretical examinations of the underlying processes of gender role socialization. <http://www.springer.com/psychology/personality+%26+social+psychology/journal/11199>

Social Forces This international journal for social research and methodology is associated with the *Southern Sociological Society*. It presents articles on such topics as mobility, class, ethnicity, gender, and education. Each issue includes book reviews. <http://sociology.unc.edu/social-forces>

Social Problems This is the official journal of the Society for the *Study of Social Problems*. *Social Problems* brings to the fore influential sociological findings and theories that have

(continued on next page)

TABLE 4–1 (continued)

the ability to help us both better understand—and better deal with—our complex social environment. <http://www.ucpressjournals.com/journal.php?j=sp>

Social Psychology Quarterly Published by the ASA, this journal covers empirical and theoretical studies related to social interaction, socialization, labeling, conformity, and attitudes. <http://spq.sagepub.com/>

Sociological Forum This official journal of the Eastern Sociological Society contains articles that link subfields of sociology to other disciplines. <http://www.blackwellpublishing.com/journal.asp?ref=0884-8971&site=1>

Sociological Inquiry Published for Alpha Kappa Delta (the undergraduate sociology honors society), it covers a wide range of sociological topics. <http://onlinelibrary.wiley.com/journal/10.1111/%28ISSN%291475-682X>

Sociological Methodology Published annually by ASA, this journal covers qualitative and quantitative methodological issues in the field of sociology. <http://onlinelibrary.wiley.com/journal/10.1111/%28ISSN%291467-9531>

Sociological Perspectives The purpose of this journal, which is sponsored by the Pacific Sociological Association, is to advance research and theory in sociology and related disciplines. <http://www.ucpress.edu/ucpjournals.php>

Sociological Theory A publication of the ASA, this journal is devoted to discussions of new and old sociological theories, theory construction, and theory synthesis. The journal also includes a section for debate and comment on recent theoretical controversies. <http://onlinelibrary.wiley.com/journal/10.1111/%28ISSN%291467-9558>

Sociology of Education Published by the ASA, this journal contains papers on human social development as well as on relations among educational institutions. <http://soe.sagepub.com/>

Symbolic Interaction Published by the Society for the Study of Symbolic Interaction, this specialized journal presents empirical and theoretical articles that take a symbolic interactionist perspective. <http://ucpressjournals.com/#about>

Theory and Society This journal presents theoretically informed analyses of social processes, providing a forum for an international community of scholars. It opens its pages to authors working at the frontiers of social analysis, regardless of discipline. The coverage ranges across a broad landscape, from prehistory to contemporary affairs, from treatments of individuals to nations to world culture, from discussions of theory to methodological critique, from First World to Third World. The effort is always to bring together theory, criticism, and concrete observation. <http://www.springer.com/social+sciences/journal/11186>

The Sociological Quarterly Sponsored by the Midwest Sociological Society, this journal presents research on recent theoretical, methodological, and empirical developments in the field of sociology. <http://onlinelibrary.wiley.com/journal/10.1111/%28ISSN%291533-8525>

Work and Occupations This journal provides a broad interdisciplinary perspective on the dynamics of the workplace and examines international approaches to work-related issues. <http://wox.sagepub.com/>

BIBLIOGRAPHIC DATABASES

While libraries remain the major outlets for academic research, books and journal articles are also available online through college or university computers where proxies have been installed. There are several search engines that provide access to these resources.

GOOGLE SCHOLAR AND *GOOGLE BOOKS* SEARCH

Google Scholar <http://scholar.google.com/> and *Google Books* <http://books.google.com> work like basic *Google* but return articles and books on the topic rather than Web sites. They are two powerful and convenient search engines for academic research. Many of the items listed link directly to the articles or books, though some may be restricted and require access from a library or university proxy. *Google Scholar* and *Google Books* results are more streamlined than results from the basic *Google* search engine because they are confined to academic research. For example, a search on "single-parent families" in basic *Google* produced 14,700,000 hits; *Google Scholar* returned more than 55,900 hits; and *Google Books* produced 1,870,000 hits.

Unlike *Google Books*, however, *Google Scholar* lists only peer-reviewed journals and will also reveal how many scholarly books and articles have cited them; a high number of citations indicates that the piece has been academically influential.

FIGURE 4–1
PROQUEST
ADVANCED SEARCH

PROQUEST

Proquest is a company that owns 46 academic databases, including search engines for specific social science disciplines. You can do a general search through your university's proxy server, but the range of sources returned will usually be too broad for most purposes. For example the general search on "single-parent families" yielded 12,800 hits. By using the Proquest advanced search you can narrow the search to specific types of documents or sources. Figure 4–1 shows this advanced search and the options available, such as language and source types. As shown in Figure 4–1, under the Advanced Search we selected "Books" and "Scholarly Journals." Under "Document types," we selected "Article," "Book,"

FIGURE 4–2
SEARCH RESULTS IN *SOCIOLOGICAL ABSTRACTS*

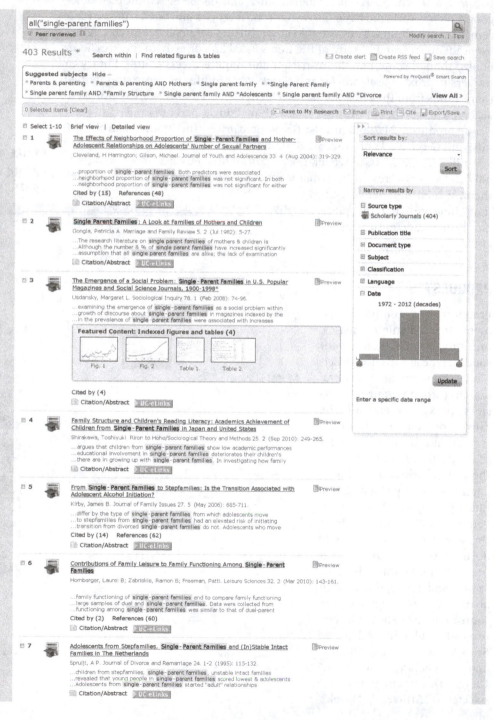

and "Book Chapter." We wanted to include the main types of sources used in a literature review. At the top of "Search Options," we checked "Peer Reviewed" in order to limit the search to scholarly books and articles. We limited the search to English language publications only. For this search, ProQuest returned 6,797 books and articles.

Of the many databases owned by Proquest one of particular use to sociologists is *Sociological Abstracts*. Proquest's *Sociological Abstracts* is a database

You can also find a useful guide to *Sociological Abstracts* developed at Indiana University at <http://www.libraries.iub.edu/index.php?pageId=2342>.

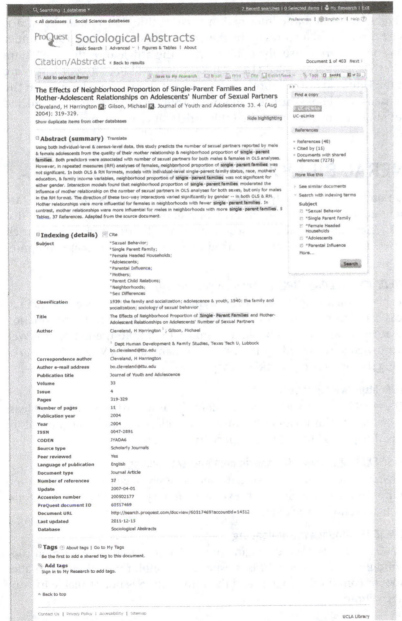

FIGURE 4–3

ARTICLE LISTING IN *SOCIOLOGICAL ABSTRACTS*

that lists all articles published in sociology journals since 1952, with brief descriptions of the articles' contents. In Figure 4–2 we present the results of a search for "single-parent families" in Proquest's *Sociological Abstracts.* Notice in Figure 4–2 there are only 403 hits for "single-parent families." The graph on the right of the screen shows in decades the trend in publishing since 1972. We can see that articles on single-parent families have increased rapidly, with fewer publications in the current decade, which is just underway at the time of this writing.

In addition to the basic information such as title, journal, and abstract, there are three useful features to the right of the page. Most important, under "Find a copy," there is usually a link to open the article directly (See Figure 4–3). In this figure it is called "UC-eLinks" but it will be different if you are not at the University of California. "References" shows the references in the article itself—the books, articles, and other sources cited. "Cited by" links to a list of publications that have cited this article since it was written.

GENERAL BIBLIOGRAPHIC SOURCES

In addition to the specifically sociological or social science sources, there are excellent general sources with information about scholarly work in all disciplines. These are available at most university libraries and through their Web sites; however, most are restricted and require a university computer or proxy.

WEB OF KNOWLEDGE (URL depends on your proxy)

The *Web of Knowledge* is a general search engine for sciences and social sciences and is useful if you want to search beyond sociology. Its information and access to articles and books are similar to Proquest, and because Web of Knowledge is owned by the same company as *EndNote* and *RefWorks,* adding the references should be easy.

JSTOR: http://www.jstor.org

JSTOR enables you to download academic journals articles that are at least five years old. This includes the most academically respectable journals in many disciplines but not many specialty journals.

LEXISNEXIS: http://www.lexisnexis.com/en-us/home.page

LexisNexis is a comprehensive data set of news, legal, government, and medical sources. It includes an extensive library on public opinion polls, which is useful for sociology papers.

WORLDCAT: http://www.worldcat.org

WorldCat serves as a search engine or as a source for locating printed copies of online information. This is especially useful if you attend a smaller school or community college and the information is not available in your college library.

SETTING UP A RECORD-KEEPING SYSTEM

Whether you record information in a desktop, laptop, or notebook, the principles are the same. Keep track of where information comes from and record the information in your own words. Keep your records organized so you can use them effectively and later create a formal bibliography for your paper.

We recommend using bibliographic software: if you obtained articles through online databases like *Sociological Abstracts,* you can use *RefWorks* or *EndNote* to put your bibliography or reference section together. These programs allow you to choose your formatting style. *EndNote* and *RefWorks* are programs that organize information on books, articles, and other sources. Each record stores information on one book or article, including author names and titles. They link up with word processing programs to automatically prepare your bibliography or footnotes. (See References and Bibliographies, pages 68–71, and Bibliographic Software, page 72, in the next chapter for more detail.)

SUMMING UP

This chapter has offered basic guidelines about navigating through the overwhelming amount of information that is accessible during your research. The goal has been to help you find a manageable number of reliable, interesting, and relevant sources focused on your topic so you can gain a better understanding of it while preparing for the next phase of writing your paper.

Citing Sources and Preparing Bibliographies

If I have seen a little further it is by standing on the shoulders of Giants.

ISAAC NEWTON
In a Letter to Robert Hooke
February 5, 1676

Knowing how to use sources is a skill: it's like playing jazz when the musician begins with a composed song, then improvises in dialogue with other musicians to take it to a higher level. This chapter is a basic introduction to the reasoning and mechanics of applying what you learn from reading sources. It includes several examples of citing and referencing various types of sources and concludes by looking at an annotated bibliography, a short critical-thinking assignment designed to help you begin your paper.

GIVING CREDIT WHERE CREDIT IS DUE— CITATIONS AND PLAGIARISM

Citing appropriate sources enhances a paper's credibility and persuasiveness: it tells the reader what was already known before you began to address a sociological question. Because research is a collective effort, academic conventions have developed to keep track of whose ideas are being borrowed so that accuracy can be checked and credit given to the proper authors. You, too, are engaging in this research process when you write a paper; and you, too, are expected to follow these conventions for identifying what you borrow from others. By acknowledging your sources in proper citations and references, you avoid plagiarism.

Plagiarism is an academic offense and can be grounds for expulsion: it is theft of intellectual property, of someone else's ideas and words. It is cheating to present another writer's words or ideas as your own. Professional scholars are similarly bound to avoid plagiarism under the guidelines in the American Sociological Association's *Code of Ethics*.

Instructors can usually detect intentional plagiarism. Their years of study have familiarized them with the articles, books, and textbooks in their fields. When a student copies this writing into a paper, instructors recognize the prose and they know it is not the student's original work. In addition, plagiarized papers do not usually resemble the student's personal writing style. Special software has now been developed to detect dishonest copying of online sources. Your instructor may ask you to submit an electronic version of your paper to a plagiarism-detecting service on campus, such as Turnitin. com, which will automatically match your paper against comparable texts in Internet databases.

Plagiarism can result from intentional cheating or mere sloppiness. To avoid unintentional plagiarism, make careful notes that respect the integrity of your sources, identifying where you found the ideas and information. One skill all students need to learn for academic writing and for most professional careers is note taking or paraphrasing. The standard rule of thumb holds that you don't need to cite common knowledge, but any presentation of an author's intellectual property must be acknowledged. *You must cite such borrowing whether you quote it directly or paraphrase it.*

When you cite borrowed information, beware of two problems: (1) Using too much of the original language without quoting, and (2) distorting the source and thereby paraphrasing it inaccurately. Following are examples of these types of problematic citations:

The original source:

The relationship between socioeconomic status and health has long intrigued social scientists. However, since its inception this research tradition has been plagued by questions of causal directionality. Namely, individuals may be sick because they are poor; alternatively, it may be their ill health itself that plunges them into poverty (e.g., through job loss due to illness).

Conley, Dalton and Neil G. Bennett. 2000. "Is Biology Destiny? Birth Weight and Life Chances." *American Sociological Review* 65(3):458–67.

1. Too much of the original source:

The relationship between socioeconomic status and health has interested social scientists for a long time. Conley and Bennett (2000), the authors of "Is Biology Destiny? Birth Weight and Life Chances," state that ". . . since its inception this research tradition has been plagued by questions of causal directionality. Namely, individuals may be sick because they are poor; alternatively, it may be their ill health itself that plunges them into poverty (e.g., through job loss due to illness)" (p. 458).

This is an example of plagiarism because, although the second sentence is a quotation, too many words from the source are used in the first sentence without quotation marks.

2. An inaccurate distortion of the original source:

According to Conley and Bennett (2000), there is a causal relationship between sociological status and health: the higher an individual's socioeconomic status, the better their health (p. 458).

This statement misrepresents the source's position.

Here is a good way to cite information from this source:

Although researchers are interested in the relationship between socioeconomic status and health, Conley and Bennett (2000) point out that it is difficult to determine whether poverty affects health or whether poor health causes poverty. (p. 458).

Do not worry about your paper lacking originality by including numerous citations. They are elements instructors expect to find when assigning quality grades; they show you have done real work. *If you are in doubt, always cite your sources.* Students often have difficulty distinguishing between common knowledge and an author's insight. For example, although the term "anomie" was coined by Durkheim, it no longer belongs exclusively to him. Over time "anomie" has become part of sociologists' working vocabularies, thus his concept is common knowledge and doesn't need to be cited. However, if you read a book or an article about the urban underclass and the author makes an important point using the concept of anomie and you use that author's point for your own paper, then you must cite him or her, but not Durkheim, as your source.

IDENTIFYING YOUR BORROWED WORDS OR IDEAS

Every time you weave someone else's idea into your paper you can quote or paraphrase the borrowed information; rely on a parenthetical citation alone to identify its source; or name the source in the text of your paper.

Quoting a source directly means extracting a word, phrase, sentence, or passage and including it into your own paper. Quoted information should be enclosed within double quotation marks or, if there are more than five lines of text, indented as a single-spaced block quotation. In regard to quoting, writing authorities Diana Hacker and Nancy Sommers explain, "In writing, keep the emphasis on your ideas; use your own words to summarize and to paraphrase your sources and to explain your points. Sometimes, however, quotations can be the most effective way to integrate a source." They go on to specify, "When to use quotations:

- ✦ When language is especially vivid or expressive
- ✦ When exact wording is needed for technical accuracy
- ✦ When it is important to let the debaters of an issue explain their positions in their own words
- ✦ When the words of an authority lend weight to an argument
- ✦ When the language of a source is the topic of your discussion" (p. 505)

If these conditions are not met, paraphrase. We chose to quote Hacker and Sommers directly because we wanted to ensure technical accuracy. We decided that paraphrasing their language might sacrifice clarity about a very important issue.

There are two minor changes allowed in a quotation, neither of which changes its meaning. These legitimate changes are illustrated in our own quotation from C. Wright Mills's *The Sociological Imagination* ([1959] 2000): "Every individual lives, from one generation to the next, in some society; . . . he [or she] lives out a biography, and . . . he lives it out with some historical sequence. By the fact of his living he contributes, however minutely, to the shaping of his society and its history; even as he is made by society and by its historical push and shove." (p. 6)

First, notice we omit some of Mills's sentence, without changing its meaning, and we indicate this omission with three spaced dots called an ellipsis. If this omission was at the end of the sentence, the ellipsis will be placed after the period making a total of four dots. Second, we are uneasy about Mills's use of "he" to refer to all humankind and want to make the language inclusive, so we add our own words "[or she]," inserting them within square brackets into Mills's quotation. Another possible addition within square brackets is the Latin word *sic,* meaning "so," which you use when you want to quote original words that contain an error such as a misspelling or racist or sexist language.

Paraphrasing means condensing the author's meaning and translating a passage into your own words. Paraphrasing forces you to think and actively understand what you have read. But if you use another's idea or fact when writing, you must give that person credit with a citation, even if you are presenting the idea in your own words.

Here is an original passage from Emile Durkheim's *Suicide* (1951), followed by two examples of poor paraphrasing and one final example of good paraphrasing":

The term "suicide" is applied to all cases of death resulting directly or indirectly from a positive or negative act of the victim himself, which he knows will produce this result. . . . This definition excludes from our study everything related to the suicide of animals. Our knowledge of animal intelligence does not really allow us to attribute to them an understanding anticipatory of their death nor, especially, of the means to accomplish it. . . . If some dogs refuse to take food on losing their masters, it is because the sadness into which they are thrown has automatically caused lack of hunger; death has resulted, but without having been foreseen. . . . So the special characteristics of suicide as defined by us are lacking. (pp. 44–45)

Following are two examples of poor paraphrasing. In the first example, the writer has shifted words in the sentences and replaced them with synonyms. The writer has not wholly condensed or translated the author's meaning; this problem is usually compounded by a failure to cite the source (in this case, Durkheim).

Example of Poor Paraphrasing:

"When some pets stop eating because their owners have left, this is caused by the unhappiness into which they have fallen, which necessarily makes them lose their appetite: the final end that ensues, however, was not anticipated. Therefore, the unique features of suicide as described by our definition are missing."

In the second example, the writer has rearranged the words but the terminology remains unchanged. As in the previous example, the writer again has not condensed or translated the passage and the problem is accentuated by the failure to cite the source.

Poor Paraphrasing Example

"Lost masters cause their sad dogs, refusing food, to lack hunger. The dogs die, not foreseeing this result. What is lacking is our special characterization of suicide as we define it."

A good paraphrase summarizes the author's idea and translates it into your own words.

Good Paraphrasing Example

According to Durkheim (1951:44–45), animals, such as abandoned dogs who starve themselves, do not commit suicide because they do not understand the connection between death and the means of causing death.

CITATIONS IN THE TEXT

If you are writing a paper on a specific aspect of suicide and you are using the insight from Durkheim quoted on page 64, there are four means of incorporating it into your paper based on how the information is presented:

+ Animals do not commit suicide (Durkheim 1951:44–45).
+ Suicide necessarily involves knowledge of the consequences. "This definition excludes . . . everything related to the suicide of animals" (Durkheim 1951:44).
+ According to Durkheim (1951:44–45) animals do not commit suicide, because committing suicide involves understanding the consequences.

✦ Durkheim (1951) argues that suicide involves knowledge of the consequences. In his words, "This definition excludes . . . everything related
to the suicide of animals" (p. 44).

Note the first two examples rely on the citation within parentheses at the
end of the sentence to identify where the information came from. The last
two examples put some parenthetical information in the text of the paper in
"a running acknowledgment" (it "runs" in the paper, and it "acknowledges"
the source). Unless you use a running acknowledgment when quoting or
paraphrasing, all the information (name, date, and page number) goes inside
one set of parentheses at the end of the paraphrased idea. If using a running
acknowledgment to paraphrase a source, place the date and page number inside parentheses immediately after you name the author. If using a running
acknowledgment to quote a source, place the date inside parentheses immediately after you name the author and the page number inside parentheses
at the end of the quotation.

When using a running acknowledgment, don't always rely on "states,"
as in "Durkheim states that . . ." Instead, experiment with using a variety
of verbs, including *maintains, contends, argues, reports, charges,* and *claims,* in a
running acknowledgement. You can also use various phrases for a running
acknowledgment, such as "according to Durkheim," or for a quotation, "in
Durkheim's words."

When choosing which four citation options to use, consider the reader.
How important is it for the reader to know immediately where the idea
comes from? Is it the idea (as in the first two examples above) or is it the
source (as in the last two examples above) that is most important?

FORMAT

The following format guidelines from the American Sociological Association
(ASA), as published in the *ASA Style Guide* (2010), describe how you should
cite paraphrased or quoted information in your paper. (Your instructor may
want you to use a different standardized format, such as the published guidelines of the American Psychological Association [APA] or of the Modern Language Association [MLA].)

In the ASA format, authors' names used in the text are followed by the
publication date in parentheses. The material inside the parentheses refers
to a source with full publication information in a page of references at the
end of the paper. The page number follows the date, or in the case of a direct
quotation, follows the quotation.

Example

Goffman (1981:180) disputes the notion that mentally ill patients are hos-
pitalized primarily for treatment. Instead, he believes that they are institutionalized so that they can be controlled.

Example

Goffman (1981) claims that the goal of hospitalization "is not to cure the patient but to contain him in a niche in free society where he can be tolerated" (p. 180).

If you don't name the author in the text of your paper, enclose the last name, year, and, if appropriate, page number(s) within parentheses at the end of the quoted thought:

Example

The treatment of the mentally ill in this country can give the impression that the goal of hospitalization "is not to cure the patient but to contain him in a niche in free society where he can be tolerated" (Goffman 1981:180).

When you write a textual analysis (see Chapter 6), you might use only one source—the book or essay you are analyzing. In this case, you need to give the publication date only once—the first time the author's name is mentioned.

Example (first mention of author in textual analysis)

Durkheim (1951) claims that suicide is not only an individual event but also a social phenomenon.

Example (after second mention of author in textual analysis)

Durkheim describes the role of social factors in suicide.

Note the page number of quotations, or of specific claims or evidence, should be indicated even after the first mention of the author.

Example

Durkheim (p. 44) defines suicide in a way that leaves all animal deaths out of his study.

Sometimes you may want to cite several authors who discuss a single idea. Then you will have a series of citations all enclosed within parentheses. The way you order them depends on the style system. Some systems prefer date order; others prefer alphabetical order, and others list authors in order of their contributions. According to the *ASA Style Guide* (2010), authors should be listed in alphabetical order by first author.

Example

Family researchers have discovered that within the first year of divorce, mothers and children undergo as much as a 30 percent decrease in family income, whereas men experience up to a 10 percent increase (Bianchi, Subaiya, and Kahn 1999; Kulik 2005; Manting and Bouman 2006).

For dual authorship, list both last names. For two or three authors, list all last names the first time you refer to the source; in subsequent citations to that source, use the first author followed by "et al." (Include all the authors' names in the References at the end of the paper.) For sources with four or more authors, use the first author followed by "et al." throughout.

Example

Employment opportunities that offer low salaries, provide no benefits (such as health insurance or pensions), have little to no job stability, and are not protected by unions or labor laws are considered of dubious benefit to workers (Ferber and Waldfogel 1996; Kalleberg et al. 1997; Mischel, Bernstein, and Schmitt 1999).

For authors with more than one publication in the same year, designate each work by adding an "a," "b," etc. to the year of publication, in the order mentioned in your paper.

Example

Individuals' subjective estimates of their life expectancy influence their morale (Mirowsky 1999a).

The impact of economic hardship on subjective life expectancy is moderated by the recency of the hardship (Mirowsky 1999b).

For citations from electronic sources, the same principles apply: include the last name of the author or the name of the organization who created the source, along with the date. This allows the reader to find the complete reference in your bibliography. See page 81 for full reference information for this electronic source.

Example

While it is common to view poverty as a permanent condition many people move in and out of poverty over periods of months and years (McKernan, et al. 2009).

If the quotation is more than five lines, present it in block-quotation form. Indent all lines five spaces from the left margin, leaving the right margin as it is throughout the text, and single-space. Quotation marks are unnecessary because the indented left margin signifies to your reader the material is quoted. The quotation on page 64 is an example of a long quotation.

NOTES

In some disciplines, sources are cited in footnotes (which appear at the bottom of each page) or endnotes (which are grouped together at the end of the paper). In sociology, however, source citations are incorporated into the text. If there are any notes, they follow the text and relay information that may be of interest to the reader but is not directly relevant to the paper's thesis. Add notes sparingly, only using them to express a comment that you feel you *must* make. And avoid using notes to interject information you are not sure how to integrate.

REFERENCES AND BIBLIOGRAPHIES

The text of your paper is followed by a record of the source materials you used to write it. Some instructors prefer a bibliography, which is a list of all the materials you consulted developing your paper. Others prefer you to use the references format used by most sociology journals, which lists only those materials actually cited in your paper. Check with your instructor to see which type of listing is preferred. The source information contained in the reference list or bibliography should allow the reader to locate all sources listed on their own.

When compiling your Bibliography or References section, list all sources alphabetically by the author's last name. Under each author's name, list works according to the year of publication, beginning with the earliest date. Do not separate the list into sections for "articles," "books," or other sources; a single list is sufficient. In the following examples, note the order of the information and how it is punctuated, <u>underlined</u> (or *italicized*, which is equivalent to underlining), and abbreviated. When formatting this section, place the heading (i.e References, Bibliography, etc.) at the left-hand margin, type it in all capital letters, and triple-space between the heading and the first source listed.

When the source you have cited has more than one author, all authors' full names should be included, in the same order in which they appear on the book's title page or after the title of the article. Alphabetize by the first author's name. The first author should be listed last name first, and the other author(s) should be listed first name first.

If no author is named for a source, then list the information in alphabetical order according to the organization responsible for its publication.

Examples of Sources with No Named Authors

Los Angeles Times. 2007. "Black Activists Search for a Constituency." February 13, p. B1.

U.S. Department of Justice's Task Force on Intellectual Property. 2006. *Progress Report of the Department of Justice's Task Force on Intellectual Property.* Washington, DC: Department of Justice.

If listing more than one work by the same author(s) replace the authors' name with a 3 em-dash (i.e. ———) after the first listing. If listing a work published by the same author(s) in the same year, identify each work by adding "a," "b," etc. to the year of publication.

Examples of multiple listings by the same author

Elias, Norbert. [1939] 1978a. *The Civilizing Process.* Vol. 1, *A History of Manners.* Translated by Edmund Jephcott. New York: Urizen.

———. 1978b. *What Is Sociology?* Translated by Stephen Mennell and Grace Morrissey. New York: Columbia University Press.

———. 2006. *Early Writings.* Translated by Edmund Jephcott. Dublin: University College Dublin Press.

Here are some general tips:

1. Is the work a book whose entire main text is written or edited by the same author or authors? If so, note that in this format titles of books are underlined or italicized in the References or Bibliography list.

Examples of Listings for Books

Seidler, Victor J. 2006. *Transforming Masculinities: Men, Cultures, Bodies, Power, Sex and Love.* New York: Routledge.

If a book was first published many years ago, include the original publication date in brackets before the more recent date.

Durkheim, Emile. [1897] 1997. *Suicide.* Translated by John A. Spaulding and George Simpson. Glencoe, IL: Free Press.

For a book that lists an editor in place of an author use the abbreviation ed. or eds. after the editors name(s).

Fetchenhauer, Detlef, Andreas Flache, Abraham P. Buunk, and Siegwart Lindenberg, eds. 2006. *Solidarity and Prosocial Behavior: An Integration of Sociological and Psychological Perspectives.* New York: Springer.

Vohs, Kathleen D. and Eli J. Finkel, eds. 2006. *Self and Relationships: Connecting Intrapersonal and Interpersonal Processes.* New York: Guilford Press.

Examples of Listings for e-Books

References for e-Books include the same information and utilize the same form as printed book with the addition of the URL and date of access.

2. Is the work an article published in a journal or periodical? In addition to the author name(s), publication year, article title, and journal title, provide the volume and issue number of the journal followed by a colon and page numbers to help your readers locate the article.

Examples of Listings for Journal Articles

Rosenfield, Sarah, Julie Phillips, and Helene White. 2006. "Gender, Race, and the Self in Mental Health and Crime." *Social Problems* 53(2):161–85.

For journals that are available in online form only include the same information as the example above, with the addition of the URL and access date. If the journal article provides a Digital Object Identifier (DOI) it is preferred that you include that instead of the URL.

Sosteric, Michael. 2012 "Gendered Ativities, Gender Difference, Gender Exclusion." *The Socjournal.* Retrieved February 15, 2013 (http://www.sociology.org/columnists/michael-sosteric/gendered-activities/)

Examples of Listings of Periodicals

When listing magazine or newspapers articles include the author name(s), publication year, article title, the date of the publication, and either the page numbers where the article can be found or the URL and access date.

Mansnerus, Laura. 2006. "Small Cities hit hard in Crime Report." *New York Times,* June 15, 2006. Retrieved September 7, 2012. (http://www.nytimes.com/2006/06/15/nyregion/15crime.html).

Genoways, Ted. 2013. "This Land Is Not Your Land: Deciding who belongs in America." *Harper's Magazine,* February, 2013. Pp. 33-41.

3. Is the work found in an edited collection or anthology? If you are referring to a specific article in the collection, the citation goes under the name of the author of the article and includes the name of the anthology and the editor(s) within the reference.

Examples of Listings for Collections:

Preissle, Judith. 2007. "Feminist Research Ethics." pp. 515–32 in *The Handbook of Feminist Research,* edited by Sharlene Nagy Hesse-Biber. Thousand Oaks, CA: Sage Publications.

Krause, Neal. 2006. "Social Relationships in Late Life." pp. 182–98 in *Handbook of Aging and the Social Sciences.* Vol. 6, edited by Robert H. Binstock and Linda K. George. San Diego: Academic Press.

4. Has the information been communicated during a class?

Example of Listing for Lecture Notes:

Lopez, David. 2012. Class lecture. October 21.

5. Does the information come from a Web site, podcast, or blog? References to these sources should include identifying information about who wrote and created the information, the Web address (URL) where it was found, and the date accessed.

Examples of Listings for Web sites:

McKernan, Signe-Mary, Caroline Ratcliffe, Stephanie R. Cellini. 2009. "Transitioning In and Out of Poverty. Washington, DC: Urban Institute. Retrieved September 12, 2012. (http://www.urban.org/publications/411956.html).

Sometimes, it is difficult to separate the original source and the Web address. Some blogs or online dictionaries and encyclopedias such as Wikipedia often give little or no information about authors or sources.

Wikipedia. 2012. "Poverty." Retrieved September 7, 2012. (http://en.wikipedia.org/wiki/Poverty).

Many government agencies, businesses, or nonprofit organizations include information about themselves at their Web sites. The URL of some do not include the familiar "www."

U. S. Bureau of the Census. 2012. "Questions and Answers: Real People, Real Questions, Real Answers." Retrieved September 7, 2012. (http://2010.census.gov/2010census/about/answers.php).

Some Web sites have no prose text, but only tables or figures. The census bureau Web site, for example, allows you to see census results on particular places or categories of people.

U. S. Bureau of the Census. 2012. "2010 Census Interactive Population Search: Nebraska." Retrieved September 7, 2012. (http://2010.census. gov/2010census/popmap/ipmtext.php).

Example of Listings for Blog Entries

Rossman, Gabriel. 2012. "Now These Are the Names, Pt 1." *Code and Culture* Blog. Retrieved February 15, 2013 (http://codeandculture.wordpress. com/page/2/).

Example of Listings for Video and Audio Online Sources

Podcasts, YouTube videos, or other video and audio sources found online should also be cited, including the type of media. Notice there is often a clearly identified author.

Kellogg, Wendy. 2012. "Social computing, mobile phones, and the developing world." Audio podcast. Retrieved September 7, 2012. (http:// www.pnas.org/site/misc/wendyKelloggPodcast.mp3).

6. Does any information in your paper come from machine-readable data files (MRDFs)? If so, you must also identify the source of the survey data. You must describe it as an MRDF and identify its producer and distributor, author, date, title, and place of origin, as well as the organization responsible for it. The codebook accompanying a data file often contains an example of a bibliographical reference for it. Machine-readable data can be tabulated into tables or analyzed with statistical techniques to draw conclusions that are not stated in words by the source. The most common form of machine-readable data is quantitative, typically from the census or surveys, but sociologists can also analyze textual data or even visual and audio data. Look for this example on the back of the codebook's title page.

Examples of Listings for MRDFs:

American Institute of Public Opinion. 1976. *Gallup Public Opinion Poll #965* [MRDF]. Princeton, NJ: American Institute of Public Opinion [producer]. New Haven, CT.: Roper Public Opinion Research Center, Yale University [distributor].

The Advertising Archives, "Sample of '1910s Collection.'" Retrieved September 7, 2012. (http://www.advertisingarchives.co.uk/?service= category&action=show_content_page&language=en&category=4&pid= 49).

BIBLIOGRAPHIC SOFTWARE

Many writers prefer to use bibliographic software to simplify keeping track of sources, formatting them in papers, and preparing bibliographies. Packages such as *EndNote* are available at college bookstores or through software vendors, while others such as *RefWorks* are subscribed to by some institutions, usually through their libraries. These packages enable you to create your own data set of books and articles that you can enter by hand or download from online sources, including many college or university library online catalogs. Bibliographic Web sites such as *Google Scholar*, the *ISI Web of Knowledge*, or *JSTOR* allow you to export citations directly into your bibliographic software. Often the same books or articles are used in different papers for different courses, so you can gradually build up a useful list for future papers. When you are writing the paper, you can enter a code for a book or article, typically the author's last name and year of publication, or use the software to insert the code as part of a Cite-While-You-Write capacity. Some word-processing programs like *Microsoft Word* are designed to interface with bibliographic software. When the paper is completed, the software can construct your bibliography according to the format you select, alphabetize it, and place it at the end of your paper. If you have the appropriate information for each source, there is little worry about how to handle the different kinds of sources, such as anthologies, unpublished dissertations, or Web sites. It does the work for you. Such software requires an initial time investment to learn the program, but once you master the basics and continue adding books and articles as you progress, the tedious work of creating bibliographies is greatly reduced.

SAMPLE ANNOTATED BIBLIOGRAPHY

Your instructor may assign one or more annotated bibliography entries at the beginning of your paper project or as an independent assignment. An annotated bibliography entry is a special kind of note taken on a source. This assignment is intended to get you started by forcing you into thinking about how you will answer your paper's question; it will also help you begin to accumulate evidence to support your thesis.

Some instructors give simple instructions for the annotation: "Write several sentences describing one source from a library database or the Internet about your topic." Here is, for example, a student's informal annotation about a report from the National Community Investment Fund: "Talks about the direct benefits of Employer Assisted Housing programs and how they treat the problem rather directly and have more positive effects than just giving workers a place to live, such as how it makes it so they can afford to live closer to where they work, helping them to maintain a stable job."

Other annotated bibliography assignments are more formal. One common assignment requires you to write a short paragraph analyzing a source and noting specific kinds of information about it. This information can include a complete identification of the publication, the authority and credentials of the author, the author's thesis, the author's evidence, the author's purpose in writing, and the author's audience.

EXAMPLE OF AN ANNOTATION FOR A PRINT SOURCE

Ocampo, Beverly Weidmer, Gene A. Shelley, and Lisa H. Jaycox. 2007. "Latino Teens Talk About Help Seeking and Help Giving in Relation to Dating Violence." *Violence Against Women* 13(2):172–89.

Esteemed social scientists Ocampo, Shelley, and Jaycox analyze dating violence among Latino youth. Rather than specify what was meant by "violence" or "date," the survey asked respondents if they had experienced violence with a date. The authors assert that teens subjected to dating violence may be more likely to seek help and support from friends than from medical professionals. Unfortunately, the type of help and support that friends provide may lead to negative consequences. For example, friends may tend to blame the victim for the abuse thereby resulting in the victim staying in the abusive relationship. Through survey and focus data on 1,655 Los Angeles teens, the researchers show that Latino youth are more likely to confide in their friends than medical professionals. The authors argue that teens must be taught skills about how to help friends experiencing dating violence because it is likely victims will continue to mistrust health-care professionals.

EXAMPLE OF AN ANNOTATION FOR A WEB DOCUMENT

U. S. Chamber of Commerce. 2012. "Do <u>something</u> about it!" Retrieved April 6, 2012. (http://www.uschambersmallbusinessnation.com/take-action/issue/energy).

This statement on "Where We Stand" by the U. S. Chamber of Commerce advocates reliance on all sources of energy with minimal government regulation. In terms of "What's Happening Now," they emphasize building the Keystone XL Pipeline to bring oil from Canada to Texas would create jobs and reduce the nation's reliance on foreign countries. They criticize federal government environmental regulation for ignoring the effect of regulations on business and jobs.

SUMMING UP

Students sometimes complain that the tedium of properly citing sources is merely compulsive and distracts from learning. But it is important to remember the reasoning behind this scholarly convention. As the chapter stated at the outset, all scholarship from a freshman exercise to a specialized monograph builds on the work of others. Not only do the authors of the works we build upon deserve their credit, but we can show our own contribution by distinguishing our ideas and evidence from theirs. Using the conventions of scholarly writing can be challenging at first, but it becomes easier over time. Achieving a high degree of competence is attainable for all students, and producing a well-formatted paper can become a source of pride. The real fun is just about to start—thoroughly reading, taking notes, organizing information, and hopefully reaching that "Aha" moment when you feel that you've really learned something.

P | A | R | T

3

Writing from Various Data Sources

As to Holmes, I observed that he sat frequently for half an hour on end, with knitted brows and an abstracted air, but he swept the matter away with a wave of his hand when I mentioned it. "Data! data! data!" he cried impatiently. "I can't make bricks without clay."

DR. WATSON IN SIR ARTHUR CONAN DOYLE'S
"Adventure of the Copper Beeches"

The goal of a sociology paper is to frame an interesting sociological question that you will answer with data. But where will the data come from?

There is no one answer. As we indicated earlier, sociology is diverse. Data may be gathered from many sources and by several methods. The next four chapters present guidelines for writing papers based on four data sources: textual analysis (Chapter 6), general research (Chapter 7), quantitative research (Chapter 8), and qualitative research (Chapter 9). They reflect the most typical writing assignments in sociology classes, and they use or modify the formats described earlier: essay and journal (see Chapter 2). As a student, you will be writing different kinds of papers, not only in

different academic disciplines, but even within each discipline. Being a well-educated person is not only about writing well in general, but also in writing different kinds of papers well. In just about any professional career, you will be called on to write different sorts of prose for different purposes and different audiences. It is hoped that this book will give you some of the facility to become proficient in several writing modes.

Therefore, we begin with writing a paper on sociological texts. We learn to write in part by studying other writing. In Chapter 6 we explain how to write a textual analysis of a book or a critique of a journal article. Both involve the process of explication—summarizing, analyzing, and evaluating your source(s)—a process that requires and strengthens critical thinking skills.

Then in Chapter 7 we discuss how to write a general research paper. Although you may be familiar with this type of paper from other classes, we offer some tips for improving your skills in reviewing sociological literature, taking notes, working with source materials, and mastering the writing process itself.

In Chapter 8 we explain how to write a quantitative research paper. Unlike the general research and textual analysis papers that use the three-part essay format the quantitative paper uses the journal format (see Chapter 2), and, therefore, is divided into four sections. In writing the first section, the literature review, you use techniques described in earlier chapters. That is, you search for appropriate sources using the library and the Internet, you critically analyze those sources, and finally you synthesize them to create a literature review. The literature review sets the stage for the development of your hypothesis, and lays the foundation for the other three sections of your paper: methods, results, and discussion.

In Chapter 9 we discuss how to do a qualitative research paper, focusing on writing an ethnographic study. Your goal in writing an ethnographic research paper is to describe the social world through the eyes of the participants in everyday settings.

To help you in writing all these papers based on different data sources, we include an annotated sample paper, written by an undergraduate sociology student, at the end of each chapter in Part 3. The sample papers illustrate our guidelines. You can match them up with your own papers and use our marginal comments to check what you have written yourself. Because no paper is perfect (not even published ones!), when reading the sample student papers, it's important to pay special attention not only to what was done correctly but also to what could be improved. It is the best way to grow as a writer.

The Textual Analysis Paper

The world isn't just the way it is. It is how we understand it, no? And in understanding something, we bring something to it, no? Doesn't that make life a story?

YANN MARTEL
Life of Pi

You may be assigned a paper asking you to analyze an article, book, or portion of a book—for example, Max Weber's *The Protestant Ethic and the Spirit of Capitalism* or Erving Goffman's *The Presentation of Self in Everyday Life*. We call this method textual analysis because the text itself is the data on which your paper is based. Your paper is *about* the text, not about the text's subject matter. For example, a textual analysis of Durkheim's *Suicide* might *analyze* his theory of suicide or his use of statistical data to study suicide, not suicide itself. A textual analysis explains the author's main points and how they are connected, and offers a critique of the argument. This process, called explication, dissects and examines the different components of the author's work and then reassembles it. An analogy is disassembling a car engine, explaining the parts and how they work together, and then evaluating whether the car is a good buy or a lemon.

Mastering the skill of explication will help you write a better textual analysis paper. But perhaps just as important, this skill will help you more clearly evaluate the books and articles you encounter in your academic career. Practicing textual analysis sharpens one's ability to think and write through the process of examining how other thinkers think and write, just as aspiring basketball players learn from game films of LeBron James or Diana Taurasi.

ASKING QUESTIONS ABOUT THE TEXT

In a textual analysis, the text is not only your data but also the source of the question your paper addresses. Your question will arise from the author's ideas and arguments presented in the text and from your analysis of them. Your question is a means for discussing the thesis or logic of the argument, the type and credibility of the evidence, the soundness of the conclusion, and the fundamental assumptions of the argument. Here are three main areas generally addressed in a textual analysis:

SUMMARY

What is the author saying? Summarizing involves reviewing and condensing the author's main points. It is sometimes not as easy as it seems. It requires seeing the entire book, not just the facts presented. For example, Durkheim's *Suicide* is not just about the relationship between religious denominations and suicide, but about how social structure helps explain what is sometimes considered the most private of individual acts, the taking of one's life.

To see the whole picture of a book, study any preface, introduction, or conclusion, and the first and last chapters of a book. Read through and think about the table of contents. What is the reasoning behind having chapters organized the way they are? Read through the section headings of the entire book. They usually give clues about what the author thinks is important. Durkheim's table of contents reveals the logic of his argument. He first considers and critiques nonsocial explanations of suicide. Then he delineates different kinds of social causation of suicide to elaborate his fundamental point that social causes matter. Finally, he generalizes about what "social" means when explaining suicide in social terms.

How does this author deal with one important sociological concept or issue in this text? Rather than analyzing all the ideas the author presents you can focus in depth on one significant aspect of the text. If you are reading Durkheim's *Suicide*, you might want to focus on just one type of suicide, perhaps egoistic suicide. "Why is family so important to egoistic suicide? What evidence does he use to support his claims about it?"

ANALYSIS

Analysis involves going beyond what the author says. It means looking at relationships: between evidence and conclusions, between concepts in the text, and between the concepts in the work being analyzed and other texts.

What devices does the author use to convince the reader that he or she is correct? One of the general skills students should learn in college is to analyze the devices that authors—all authors, not just sociologists or academic writers—use to convince a reader. All of these have their place in writing, but all can be misused. The key here is to learn to identify what an author is doing to persuade the reader to understand, identify with, and support his or her conclusions.

Logical reasoning. The most common form of logical reasoning is the syllogism—an *if . . . then* statement. Here the author seeks to convince you there is a logical connection between something you already believe and something he or she wants you to believe. For example, Durkheim essentially argues that if social groups have an effect on whether a person feels a moral wholeness and if moral wholeness influences whether a person might commit suicide, then there must be a relationship between social groups and suicide. Logical reasoning can also take the form of an analogy, with something the author wants you to understand in a certain way being compared with something familiar to you. For example, Durkheim argues that suicide is a form of deviance, just as crime is a form of deviance. Both stem from an absence of purpose or ideals, or "anomie." There are many other logical devices that authors use, all of which follow identifiable rules in relating elements of an argument.

Anecdote. Anecdotes are little stories used to illustrate a point. For example, a paper could begin with a story about a particular criminal or crime victim, with the unstated assumption that the story is representative of all criminals or victims. A single statistic can be used anecdotally to add credence to a paper. Anecdotes can bring a paper to life, but they do not substitute for systematic evidence.

Appeal to authority. It is common to demonstrate that someone the reader respects agrees with the author's perspective. This can be either an "expert," whose knowledge of a subject qualifies him or her for respect, or a luminary, whose social status or position makes the person believable.

Methodologically informed study. This device answers a very specific and empirically verifiable question, such as "Are Catholics less likely to commit suicide than Protestants?" A study designed according to the rules of an academic method is conducted for this purpose. Durkheim rested his case on a quantitative study comparing suicide rates in Protestant and Catholic areas of Europe. Other researchers have studied suicide with ethnographic, or comparative and historical methods.

Rhetorical virtuosity. This includes a number of devices that can be employed to convince a reader by using the writer's language skills. A well-turned phrase or metaphor, such as *baby boom, sensuous sixties, animal rights,* or *law and order* may sound poetic because of its selection of words. Scientific jargon can give unscientific ideas the sound of authority. Big words or convoluted sentences can make the author sound intelligent and knowledgeable. Humor, satire, or irony can be used to make opposing views sound ridiculous.

What is important is that the student understands what the author is doing and is able to analyze the devices being used.

EVALUATION

How well does the author answer his or her question and verify that answer? This is the realm of criticism (both positive and negative). It logically comes last. You can't judge a text until you comprehend what the author is doing and how he or she does it. Evaluation is also the most subjective stage. While

> "When a truth is necessary, the reason for it can be found by analysis, that is, by resolving it into simpler ideas and truths until the primary ones are reached."
>
> Gottfried Leibniz

an instructor can grade how well you summarize or analyze a work, what you think of the work is your personal opinion. However, the line between analysis and evaluation is sometimes blurred, and an instructor may legitimately fault you for basing your evaluation on an inaccurate summary or sloppy analysis. Instructors also have different ideas about how much evaluation they want. Some want students to express their opinions about a text; others just want a summary and/or analysis. Evaluation involves asking the following questions:

Is the argument of the text clear? Is it clear what question the text is attempting to answer? Are the definitions precise and unambiguous? Are the concepts appropriate to the questions addressed? Are the conclusions explicitly presented or implicit for the reader to decipher? This dimension of evaluation concerns the summary. If the summary is easy to write, the text rates high on this criterion. Sometimes the most influential authors' writings, especially by a field's founders, require the most work to summarize.

Does the author make valid assumptions? Identifying and evaluating an author's assumptions are two of the intellectual skills often demanded in sociological theory classes. Authors necessarily make assumptions about the way the world works. For example, some theories assume that human beings act primarily on the basis of material self-interest, whereas others assume that people are motivated by the need for social approval. Some theories treat society as the aggregation of individuals, assuming that all social behavior can be reduced to individual behavior. Others assume that there are factors such as social class that can only be understood at the level of society. Once an author's assumptions are identified, the plausibility of those assumptions can be determined.

How well does the text use evidence? Does the evidence adequately support the conclusions? If the text is based on a specific study, how well was the study performed? If the evidence is less systematic, does it seem to be fairly drawn or carefully selected to favor the author's point of view? This is where many beginning students feel ill equipped because they have not been thoroughly trained in methods and may feel they don't know enough about a topic to gauge whether the evidence is selective. Despite these limitations, some instructors encourage students to try this type of evaluation. Most students should have some sense of whether the evidence adequately supports the conclusion.

Are the conclusions and implications supported by other works? Comparing the text being studied with other texts is common when other scholars have written about the same subject and is especially useful when those works have achieved a sort of orthodoxy. Durkheim's observations that different religions have different suicide rates because they have different degrees of social solidarity have frequently been put to additional empirical testing, with some results validating Durkheim's findings and others challenging them. The debate, nonetheless, has focused on the particulars of Durkheim's analysis more than his general insight that the causes of suicide are at least as much social as they are individual.

Is the craftsmanship of the writing sound? Do the parts fit into a whole? Is the prose understandable? Do the ideas flow smoothly? Craftsmanship is the theme of this book. If you were grading the text according to our criteria, how would it stand up?

Remember different instructors have different tastes concerning how much evaluation they want and along what criteria. Some want you to focus on the text itself, while others want the text evaluated relative to other works. Some emphasize an evaluation of the logic, others of the evidence, and still others emphasize evaluation of the assumptions. Make sure you understand the instructor's expectations.

COMPARE–CONTRAST ASSIGNMENTS

Instructors often ask students to examine the work of two or more authors to see what ideas, logics, and methods they have in common and how they might contrast with one another. If you are asked to compare and/or contrast two authors' works or two works by the same author, you must start by identifying a common topic under consideration and use it as the basis for your question. How do these two works deal with an issue that is central to each? Note the advice to find a common topic would not apply if the instructor asks you to enumerate all the points in common and all the points in contrast.

Any or all of these three aspects—summary, analysis, and evaluation—may be relevant to the particular work you are considering. Before you decide which questions will form the basis of your paper, you must carefully read the text. We recommend that you print the text from your computer or buy your own copy of the book so you can mark it up.

HOW TO READ THE TEXT

Before developing your question, familiarize yourself with the text. As you read, keep in mind three general tasks. First, you must *identify the main points* that are explicitly presented as parts of the argument. Second, you must *identify the author's hidden assumptions*—that is, what she or he takes for granted about how the world works and does not question or bother to justify. Third, you must *evaluate* the text, asking what is or isn't convincing about the argument. What are its problems? How could it be better? Evaluating the argument is like diagnosing which of a car's engine parts do not work and how they could work, or arguing that the whole thing should be junked and stating why.

Following is a more detailed description of the close reading required for textual analysis.

GETTING TO KNOW SOMETHING ABOUT THE TEXT

Here are some things you must find out in order to become acquainted with the text:

Who is the author? What is her or his background? This information is sometimes included in the introduction to the book. If there is no biographical information in the introduction, or if the information is insufficient, it is usually available on the Web. If the author is living and works as a professor, you can search online for his or her name, discipline, and university.

When was the text written? What was the social climate of the period? To determine when the text was written, look at the copyright date in the front of the book. If you find more than one date, the first one indicates the date of the original printing or first edition; however, translated books were written earlier than the English language edition.

To determine the historical period when the text was written, look to your introduction first. If this does not provide adequate information, a Web search should provide historical information about the author, the countries where the author lived, and sometimes details of the text's creation.

What is the polemical context? What controversial argument is being disputed? What debates was the text speaking to when it was written? To whom is the author responding? Sometimes the text will reveal the polemical context by contrasting the author's argument with other perspectives. This information may be found in the body of the text or in the preface or introduction. Sometimes it requires reading between the lines and paying attention to how the author refers to other works—for example, by drawing contrasts between her or his position and that of others. If the polemical context is not obvious, look for other books or journal articles about the author or the subject of the text. Often scholars write critiques or commentaries on others' work, especially if it is considered controversial or exemplary. This literature can be found in electronic databases (see Chapter 4). Remember, the reference librarian can help you locate sources to help you get the information you need.

READING TWICE

A useful skill to learn is how to read differently for different purposes. For example, a novel can be read faster and less critically than a textbook.

For the purposes of textual analysis, first, read for the big picture—get a feel for the text's organization and content. Pay special attention to the author's introduction, often called a preface, or to the foreword, written by an expert in the field.

After you have completed this preliminary reading, focus on the kind of question you will be addressing in your paper. If your instructor has specified a question, now is the time to consider it. Be sure you understand what information to provide, how to deeply analyze the work, and how much of your own opinion to give. If the assignment is more general decide which approach you will take: Will you analyze the text as a whole? Would you rather focus on a particular concept or aspect of the argument? Or should you compare this work with another one?

With your question in mind, reread the text carefully as this reading forms the core of your "data collection." Your goal is to understand the interconnected points that constitute the author's argument and to record these important points. Note taking during this second reading is an important step toward writing your paper and is addressed in the next section.

What are you looking for in this detailed reading? Look for the author's argument—the question the author is trying to answer and the evidence she or he uses to answer it. The following questions will assist you in identifying the author's main points and the assumptions hidden beneath them:

+ What is the author's question? For example, in *Suicide*, Durkheim asks, "What are the social factors that help explain suicide?"
+ What is the author's answer—what provides the core of the argument? What answers have other scholars given? Durkheim argues that the degree of social solidarity within groups that people belong to affects how likely they are to commit suicide. When Durkheim lived, Protestants were more likely than Catholics to commit suicide because Protestantism provided less social solidarity than Catholicism. He was trying to demonstrate that psychological explanations that emphasized individual pathology were not sufficient in determining the causes of suicide.
+ What evidence does the author offer to support this answer? Is the evidence logical or empirical or both? Does the evidence actually support the argument? As mentioned before, Durkheim used statistics on suicide rates.
+ How does the author get from point A to point B? How do the main points that you identified in your reading relate to one another? Durkheim did not present direct evidence about individual suicides, but based his conclusion on group rates. As a group Protestants were found to have more suicides than Catholics, but he had no evidence that any particular Protestant suicide victim was feeling more suicidal than any particular Catholic.
+ What are the assumptions? What does the author take for granted, points without which the argument couldn't be made? Some examples of fundamental assumptions are that people have free will, our social order constitutes the normal state of affairs, and free enterprise benefits everyone. Durkheim assumed that people have a deep need for social solidarity and that the emptiness felt without such solidarity could lead to such a desperate act as suicide.

As you engage in this second reading, you may want to adjust your questions. For example, if you planned on analyzing the text as a whole you may now discover that for this paper that task is too broad, resulting in a weak analysis. Conversely, you may discover that it is not possible to discuss one concept without analyzing the text as a whole or you might need to explain this text without comparing or contrasting it with another work. If your focus is too narrow, the reader might not understand your analysis.

TAKING NOTES

As C. Wright Mills explains in his appendix, "On Intellectual Craftsmanship," to *The Sociological Imagination* ([1959] 2000), "You will have to acquire the habit of taking a large volume of notes from any worth-while book you read" (p. 199). Taking notes is a personal skill that varies from student to student.

"I could not think without writing."

Jean Piaget

Regardless of how or where they are physically recorded, carefully taken notes provide two benefits. As Mills explains, "the mere taking of a note from a book is often a prod to reflection. At the same time, of course, the taking of a note is a great aid in comprehending what you are reading" (p. 199). The first kind of note described by Mills as "a prod to reflection," can take the form of annotations: definitions, cross-references, examples, questions, or other ideas that are triggered in your mind as you read. It is your part of the dialogue you are having with the author.

In the second kind of note, Mills continues, "you try to grasp the structure of the writer's argument" (p. 199). This type of note is more objective and is a systematic restatement of all or part of the author's argument. This summarizing kind of note outlines the author's main points and the interrelationships between the points and their evidence. In general, you should paraphrase the author's original words rather than quote them. You should quote only in a few special instances (see Chapter 5).

When using the author's exact words, be sure to mark them as a quotation in your notes to ensure proper citation in your paper. You must also document paraphrases (see Chapter 5).

One challenge of note taking is to avoid repeating facts from the text. Your notes should begin the process of analysis with remarks such as "assumes individual causes matter," "rejects quantitative methods," "the opposite perspective from previous reading," or "see how suicide is treated as a form of deviance." While summarizing the text, you may also evaluate the argument or evidence, but remember to mark your ideas as your own to prevent confusing them with the author's.

ORGANIZING YOUR PAPER

Once you have read the text and made notes, the next step is to outline your analysis and plan how to present it. The essay format is more suitable than the journal format for textual analysis (see "Developing an Argument: Logic and Structure" in Chapter 2). Within the basic essay format there are a number of ways in which you can organize your paper. Here are three basic outline patterns you can use or modify:

I. *Organize the body of your paper into three main parts corresponding to the three main tasks involved in explication.*
   1. Summary: Your description of what the author is saying; the author's main points.
   2. Analysis: Your explanation of what is behind the author's argument; for example, the polemical context or debate being addressed, the author's hidden assumptions, the author's evidence, and implications of the author's points.
   3. Evaluation: Your assessment of the strengths and weaknesses of the author's argument. How well do the main points fit together? How relevant is the evidence to the points being made? How convincing are the conclusions?

II. *Organize the body of your paper into major points that assert what is most important about the text.*
   1. In your introduction, identify the most important features and state your position. You might also want to state the positions of other scholars unless your assignment excludes the use of outside sources.
   2. In the second paragraph (or section, in a longer paper), summarize one main point you want the reader to know in order to accept your point of view and provide detailed evidence from the text to support this point.
   3. Repeat in the third and fourth paragraphs or sections, presenting one more major point in each.
   4. In your conclusion, restate your claims and summarize and support your points.

III. *Organize your paper around comparing and contrasting.* There are two basic pattern combinations you can follow to compare and contrast two works:

PATTERN I	PATTERN II
A (1st author)	1 (1st point)
1 (1st point)	A (1st author)
2 (2nd point)	B (2nd author)
3 (3rd point)	2 (2nd point)
B (2nd author)	A (1st author)
1 (1st point)	B (2nd author)
2 (2nd point)	3 (3rd point)
3 (3rd point)	A (1st author)
	B (2nd author)

WRITING YOUR TEXTUAL ANALYSIS

Your goal is to logically and coherently answer the questions you have been asking about the text as you read. A review of Chapter 2 "Developing an Argument: Logic and Structure" will help. Keeping these key questions about the text in mind as you write and revise will prevent you from wandering. Remember to identify the author and text in your opening paragraph.

When writing a research paper, you must follow formal conventions for documentation. For a textual analysis, however, it is usually sufficient to indicate only in the first reference with the publication date of the text you are analyzing. Thereafter you may document quotations with the author's name and appropriate page number. When referring to an idea or argument found frequently throughout the text, the author's name alone, included in one of your own sentences, will suffice: for example, "Elias states . . ." See pages 52–54 for illustrations of these special citation formats.

A SAMPLE STUDENT PAPER

Lysa Agundez's paper was written for a course in culture and personality. The text she chose to analyze was Norbert Elias's *The Civilizing Process*. It was an appropriate choice because Elias's goal was to show how individual psyches and actions take the same shape as the social structure in which they occur. We selected Lysa's paper not only because it illustrates a concise summary of a complex sociological work but also because of its gritty and interesting subject matter.

Here Lysa attempts to show how Elias uses the sociological imagination to connect the most personal of experiences with large-scale social relations.

Lysa identified and designed her paper around two key issues in the text she analyzed. The format of her paper is a variation of the three-part essay format—in this case, a two-part format. Our comments in the margins indicate how Lysa addressed the three questions we have recommended you consider in any textual analysis: What is the author saying (summary)? What devices does the author use to convince the reader that he or she is correct (analysis)? How well does the author answer his or her question and verify the answer (evaluation)?

Demonstrating a problem many students encounter, Lysa's summary is more complete than her analysis and evaluation. Follow her paper and our remarks to see the strengths of her work and where improvements can be made.

Note: We have excluded all title pages from sample student papers in chapters 6, 7, and 9 to save space. See p. 129 in Chapter 8 for a sample title page.

OUR COMMENTS

NORBERT ELIAS ON THE DEVELOPMENT OF CIVILIZATION
THROUGH REPRESSION OF INSTINCTS

Lysa Agundez
Sociology 134
Professor Heritage

This paper will discuss the theories of Norbert Elias, who argues that the development of civilization involves a repression of instincts. The nature of this essay entails addressing two issues: (1) The stricter control of emotion and behavior developed following the Middle Ages; and (2) The relationship of shame and the structure of society. Then I will discuss Elias's distinctive contributions to investigation of the civilizing process.

Norbert Elias is a German sociologist, whose two-volume masterpiece is titled *The Civilizing Process*. The first volume, titled *The History of Manners,* is a complete presentation of basic attitude changes of European manners and morals. Examples include attitudes towards bodily functions, table manners, sexual behavior, and aggression. The second volume, titled *Power and Civility,* presents a thorough sociological analysis of the development of civilized behavior formed by the centralization of society.

The process of civilization, Elias believes, involved a progressively stricter control of emotion and habits of restraint that led to socially institutionalized frontiers of shame and emotional standards. Thus, the growth of civilization, Elias believes, involves the gradual intensification of instinctual repression over the centuries. In *The History of Manners,* Elias documents the gradual domestication of human affects and emotions from the Middle Ages to our days. His purpose is to show how the psychical makeup of modern men and women differs in significant ways from their ancestors. Compared to modern man, medieval people, Elias argues, were faced with few barriers to the acting out of affect, be that in the area of aggression, sex, at the dinner table, or in the bedroom.

1

Sidebar comments:

Notice that the title indicates that the topic is about Norbert Elias's work, not about the development of civilization as a topic in its own right. That is why it is a textual analysis paper, not a general research paper.

Note that Lysa plans to address only two issues; it is not required for the student to have three main points.

The second paragraph begins Lysa's summary of her first point. Lysa's paper should include a bibliography or reference page, including the publication information on both volumes.

While it is essential to attribute Elias's ideas, Lysa should vary the terminology. After using "believe" twice, she wisely uses other terms in the rest of the paragraph— "documents . . . show . . . argues . . ." She could have used yet another term for the second "believe," such as "maintains," "asserts," "explains," and so forth.

Lysa appropriately numbers the pages of her paper.

Lysa's use of these examples as evidence for her explication would be strengthened by citing their sources from Elias's text. In fact, with material as colorful as this, direct quotation would liven up the scholarly discussion and keep the reader's interest.

To prove his point, Elias turns to various etiquette and manners books that have been steadily written and very widely read since the days of Erasmus of Rotterdam. Written mainly for members of European court society, these books exemplify right and wrong behavior. Systematically comparing their changing content over time, Elias takes them as guides to the changing lifestyles and sense of propriety on the passing historical scene.

Many of the teachings of Erasmus's book of manners would be taken for granted by most children today. For example, medieval writers tell their readers in quest for refinements of manners that one should not gnaw a bone and then throw it back into the common dish, that diners should not wipe their nose on their hands or spit into the plate, nor poke in their mouth, nor scratch themselves while eating. These elementary rules were necessary for fifteenth-century feudal nobles, who, in fact, ate with their hands, threw bones to dogs gathered around the table, dipped their fingers in common dishes, and drank from a common goblet.

By the sixteenth century, however, the time of Erasmus, standards became gradually more demanding, and people more self-conscious of their public manners. As time went on, eating habits gradually became more refined. People began to use forks instead of searching with pieces of bread for chunks of meat in the common pot. They were taught that they should use their knives unobtrusively so as not to threaten their neighbors at the table.

Erasmus, in an effort to teach "civility" to the nobility and the aspiring bourgeoisie, did not limit his advice to table manners. With a lack of embarrassment that might seem gross to modern sensibilities, he attempted to teach his public the circumstances in which spitting, farting, urinating, or defecating in public might or might not be defensible.

Lysa does a good job of summarizing the advice offered in the etiquette books that serve as Elias's data. More direct quotations would provide the reader with a stronger sense of the materials he used to reach his conclusions.

Spitting, for instance, was a common "natural" bodily function in the Middle Ages. As a matter of fact, it was even considered a custom and was commonplace in the courts of feudal lords. The only major restriction imposed then was that "one should not spit on or over the table but under it" (I, p. 156). In the sixteenth century, people were provided with spittoons. And in our age, the "need" for spitting in public has been altogether abolished.

Farting in public also became prohibited over the civilizing process. In the Middle Ages, it was considered unhealthy to "hold back wind" (I, p. 130). It was better to be emitted with a noise than to be held back. Gradually, however, the feeling of embarrassment increased, and it was instructed to calm your body by farting only while covering the sounds with coughs, or, if one was in a holy place, to press your buttocks together. By the eighteenth century, farting, like spitting, was abolished.

People furthermore used to urinate and defecate in public, and polite etiquette guides simply taught their readers that one should avoid looking at people engaging in these activities. Even in the Palace of Versailles, people used to relieve themselves in corridors and on staircases. As a result, a huge consumption of perfume at the court was required to hide the offensive odors in the palace.

To Elias, these changes are not just curious: they indicate basic changes in the ways human beings perceive themselves and use their bodies in relation to those of others. People now began to mold themselves and others more self-consciously and deliberately than was the wont and use of the Middle Ages. Much of what we now consider "second nature" was the result of a century-long process of gradual domestication. As external restraint against personal emissions gave way to self-restraint, an "invisible wall" gradually grew up between one human body and another.

Elias also documents complementary movements involving sleeping habits and sexuality. Here, also, the public became distinguished from the private sphere. In medieval society it was quite normal for many people,

3

It is acceptable to use language normally considered vulgar to describe a historical situation, especially if it is used in the text; however, if it makes you uncomfortable, or it might be offensive to your instructor, adopt a euphemism instead.

"Polite etiquette guides" is redundant; etiquette involves politeness. *Redundancy* means unnecessarily repeating a thought, often by using different words that mean the same thing.

The contrast between the reader's likely image of Versailles as a glamorous place and Lysa's discussion of perfume stimulates reader interest. Concrete details like this generally engage the reader if they have a clear connection to the paper's conceptual message, as this example does.

even strangers, to spend the night in one room and even to share the same bed. Today, however, the bedroom has become privatized and separated from the rest of social life.

Moreover, in the Middle Ages it was customary for guests at a wedding to terminate the proceedings by undressing the bride and groom who were then obliged to consummate the marriage in the presence of the assembled company. By the late Middle Ages, the custom gradually changed to the extent that the couple was placed on the bed fully dressed. After this period, sexual life was concealed and dismissed behind the scenes altogether.

Elias argues that these examples of changes in sexual behavior, along with those illustrating changes in standards of self-restraint, mark the advance in the threshold of shame. Noting that restrictions of various kinds surround the elimination of natural functions in many societies, both "primitive" and "civilized," he concludes that the fears of natural elimination and the feeling of shame and repugnance in which it is expressed do not originate from a rational understanding of the origins of certain diseases, as one might think. Actually, our understanding of their dangers is attained only in the nineteenth century, at a very late stage in the civilizing process.

Elias argues that our feelings of distaste and shame are based on changes in the ways people live together in the structure of society. He discusses these changes in social structure at length in *Power and Civility,* in which he announces:

> . . . [T]he civilizing of conduct and the corresponding transformation of human consciousness and libidinal make-up cannot be understood without tracing the process of state formation, and within it the advancing centralization of society which first finds particularly visible expression in the absolute form of life (II, p. 8).

4

Marginal notes:

Overall, Lysa makes good use of the transitional words and phrases discussed in Chapter 2. In this case, "Moreover" signals that she is building on the previous paragraph.

Since "threshold of shame" is a special term that conveys one of Elias's key concepts, it would be good to define or explain it here.

This is where Lysa begins her summary of the second point she introduced in the opening paragraph.

Because of this quotation's length, Lysa has appropriately indented and single-spaced the paragraph.

Here is a good example of the importance of including full publication information for references: when searching for more information on this quotation, we could not find it on page 8 of our copy of the second volume. Perhaps Lysa used a different edition, but, since no publication information is provided, we cannot tell for sure.

Despite the cumbersome formulation, Elias's basic thesis is unexpectedly simple and convincing: as society became more centralized, individuals came into close contact and began to exercise greater self constraint—"more affect control," in Elias's jargon.

For example, Elias believes feudal knights behaved like powerful and uninhibited children. These knights vigorously (and often violently) engaged in self-defense and self-gratification, clearly demonstrating minimal manners. "What was lacking," Elias observes of this impulsive personality, "was the invisible wall of affects which seems now to rise between one body and another, repelling and separating" (II, p. 256). The courtiers who congregated later in absolutist courts were far more careful types; relying now on central royal authority for physical protection, they vied (rarely violently) for influence and advancement. Consequently, the feudal knights increasingly had to regulate their behavior to secure protection and promotions.

Furthermore, crude feudal "courtoisie" was replaced by a more exacting code as courtiers strived to maintain their status, fending off the bourgeoisie below. The threshold of shame and embarrassment rose and rational forethought became a more important guide to conduct; bodily functions hidden, spontaneous impulses suppressed and more elaborate proprieties established. Henceforth those "invisible walls" were everywhere, creating private selves who anxiously calculated their actions, thereby increasing self-control over passions and emotions.

Elias's ideas are similar to those of other authors, such as Sigmund Freud. So what makes for the distinctive contribution of this book? It is Elias's true leap of the sociological imagination when searching for data through which this process might be documented; his use of etiquette manuals was very creative, and his research was very thorough. Even though his work was published forty years after it was written, it is not at all outdated. In fact, it is encompassing and stands complete today.

5

> When Lysa claims that Elias's thesis is "convincing," it sounds like she is ready to begin an evaluation of the text. However, she continues her summary without giving the reader any evidence of *why* she believes the thesis is convincing.

> To strengthen her paper Lysa could have started analyzing Elias's method of convincing the reader to accept his point of view. Lysa's evaluation of the text should follow her analysis. This is where she might tell the reader why she believes Elias's basic thesis is "convincing."

Including Thomas's critique strengthens Lysa's paper by showing she is aware of what others have written about Elias. Unfortunately, no citation is given, so the reader is unable to judge his credibility or to further investigate his assessment.

One might argue that Elias's focus is too narrow. Elias chose to focus only on the transformation of people from the Middle Ages to our times and has eschewed the occasion for a comparative treatment of the subject. As Keith Thomas (1978) has pointed out, Elias says next to nothing about the world of Greco-Roman antiquity in which a similar process had surely taken place, even though the results of that process were largely lost during the Dark Ages. There is next to nothing in the book about other high civilizations, such as those of Asia, in which one can discern similar trends. But these are, after all, minor matters. One can hardly reproach an author who has given so much for not having written a world history of manners.

While the conclusion is the most appropriate place for the author's personal feelings, it should also bring the reader full circle by summarizing or drawing conclusions about the work or its significance.

In conclusion, I was very happy that I got to work on such an interesting topic. I think one can learn from Elias's detailed method of research—looking in countless manners books and presenting the material the way things really happened and then giving a thorough sociological explanation of civilization.

C H A P T E R
S E V E N

The General Research Paper

Knowledge is power only if man knows what facts not to bother with.

ROBERT STAUGHTON LYND

The difference between a paper and a collection of facts and ideas is form. The form of a paper—the way it is organized between sentences, paragraphs, and sections—makes sense of otherwise disconnected rambling.

Once you have refined a question, read about your topic, taken effective notes, and are ready to write, how do you transition into creating a well-organized, convincing paper? This chapter will review the basic steps in creating the general research paper, starting with identifying your research topic, moving through taking notes and finally crafting your paper.

Early in the writing process you need to identify your research question or theme. The theme is a statement that answers your question; it is what the paper is *about*, not just defining the topic. For example, the sample student paper in this chapter is about how country and western music expresses white identity. The implicit question is whether country and western music expresses any racial identity analogous to the way that rap music often expresses African American identity. Notice that there is more than one plausible alternative answer to the question, as many Americans, including country and western fans, maintain that country and western music has no racial identity. So the author, Mayank Chawla, must present evidence to support her argument that it does have a racial identity. Consider forming a tentative answer to your question and managing it in a separate document where you can revise it and take notes while still keeping it close at hand as you work on the paper.

REVIEWING THE SOCIOLOGICAL LITERATURE

The first step is to find what is already known about your topic. As reviewed in Chapter 4, finding and navigating through information are two of the most important skills a student can learn. Assume that you have found sources that address your question. How do you begin taking notes without being overwhelmed? Reviewing the literature will help you in two ways.

First, it will help you refine your question. How has the question been framed before? For example, you might want to know why jails are full of people convicted of drug violations. You may begin the query wanting to know why so many people have abused drugs but find that many scholars have approached the question asking why courts have steadily toughened the penalties for drug violations. Or you might find that much of the literature about drug use focuses on why some people use illegal drugs more frequently than others instead of questioning why so many people in general use them. With this information in mind you may decide to fine-tune your question. Remember that you must be able to find sufficient evidence to support the answer you will propose, and it must be specific enough to be researchable within the time frame of your assignment.

Second, reviewing the literature will help you identify books and journal articles that contain reports of research into the question you will address in your paper. The quality of your paper will depend on how thoroughly you locate this research; it is the "data" you will use to support your thesis.

TAKING NOTES FOR THE GENERAL RESEARCH PAPER

Unlike the notes taken for a textual analysis (see pages 119–126) that attempt to outline and restate the text's main argument, notes for a general research paper are taken with the goal of finding evidence for your thesis. As C. Wright Mills explains in "On Intellectual Craftsmanship," in *The Sociological Imagination* ([1959] 2000):

> Rather than read entire books, you will very often read parts of many books from the point of view of some particular theme or topic in which you are interested. . . . Therefore, you will take notes that do not fairly represent the books you read. You are *using* this particular idea, this particular fact, for the realization of your own projects. (P. 199)

While there is no single correct way to take notes there are some general principles to keep in mind. First, keep in mind the question you are addressing, the answer you expect to offer, and alternative answers that you will be arguing against. Ask what answer the source you are taking notes on might offer, what information supports your answer (or makes you rethink it), and what information supports other answers. It is helpful to write down key words or topics describing or relating to your notes that you can find quickly, perhaps at the top of the document or page. For example, if you are writing about homelessness and expect to organize the paper into sections on causes, effects, and solutions, you might use those terms to organize your notes and later your paper.

Second, unless you plan to use a direct quote, summarize the book or article in your own words. This will reduce the potential for plagiarism. Remember, borrowing words or ideas from an author requires proper attribution (see Chapter 5). Another advantage of summarizing in your own words is that it increases your comprehension of the material.

Third, think while you are reading. After reading several sources, you should begin to see patterns emerging about how a topic like homelessness is viewed and what major points of agreement and disagreement exist among scholars. For example, some work on homelessness focuses on the characteristics of the homeless themselves, emphasizing substance abuse, mental illness, or family background. Others emphasize the structural forces, such as housing costs, lack of services, or welfare reform. When you have a sense of how a body of knowledge regarding a topic is organized, you can make note of where readings fit into the field.

Finally, write your own interpretations and reactions as you take notes. These annotations can be an extensive analysis or they can be a comment like "A very valuable source." They can also be an observation about the text's relation to other sources, such as "A useful rebuttal to Garcia." Some people like to identify their own reactions with a symbol such as an asterisk (*).

HIGHLIGHTING AND WORKING WITH SOURCE MATERIALS

Although highlighting or annotating a text while reviewing are no substitute for taking notes, these practices can be very helpful. Consider trying pens in several different colors, one for each subtopic. For example, the student researching single-parent families used one color for statistical data, another for information about legal resources and regulations, and a third color for information about children in these families. This visually separates your subheadings for easier identification. Write your color-coding key somewhere you can locate readily.

Another note-taking tip is writing the author's name or the title of the article on the page you are highlighting and annotating. You should have already collected the bibliographic data in one location, but this will enable you to match up the information, and prevent you from saving the entire article if you are only using one page.

Many students discover that computer files, photocopies, and printouts accumulate quickly during the research process. Rearranging and shuffling pages into different categories can be useful. Mills explains that this "rearranging" process is "one way to invite [the sociological] imagination. . . . You simply dump out heretofore disconnected folders, mixing up their contents and then re-sort them" (p. 212). If you do this on the computer, however, make copies in a different directory and keep track of the originals.

Following Mills's advice that writers play around with their files, rearranging them and developing new file headings can lead to new insights about a research question. For example, files on a paper focusing on divorce originally might have been labeled "strain of modern life," "financial stress,"

Learn more about annotating or note taking on PDF files at http://en.wikipedia.org/wiki/Portable_Document_Format#Annotation.

Computer Tip: Some people take all their notes in one computer file and us the search function to organize them. If you do this remember to search for variations of topic or terms you might have used in your notes, (for example African American, African-American, Afro-American, black, etc). If you only search one term you will miss others.

Computer Tip: Hyperlinking common terms throughout your notes will allow you to move quickly through your various files.

"disagreement over raising children," and "adultery." But upon reading the files, the writer may find the material fit better in categories like "class differences," "attitudes toward women's roles," "legal changes," and "demographic change." The process of shuffling and reorganizing your files often will leave you with a clearer understanding of the significance of your collected data and better prepare you to organize your paper.

WRITING THE GENERAL RESEARCH PAPER

Remember from Chapter 2, there is nothing magic about the number three. If your paper has two points, you can write it in two sections. If your paper has four points you can write it in four sections.

Though general research papers can take many formats, we will address the three-part essay format. If you would like to follow another format, we advise discussing it with your instructor or teaching assistant.

Once the writing stage has been reached, the first step is to finalize the paper's thesis—the paper's main point that includes a simple statement answering the paper's research question. The next step is to identify supporting points. For example, a research question may ask how sociologists explain when and where social movements arise, and the corresponding thesis might be that they cannot agree on the answer to the question. The supporting points could then be the three major perspectives held by sociologists of social movements (resource mobilization, framing, and political opportunity) and how they conflict.

In contrast to different theoretical perspectives, a paper could be organized by different stages of a social process. For example, a paper about how family members share social and material resources might be organized into three stages of life: childhood, adulthood, and old age, and how resources are shared at each stage. The three points could also be three aspects of the main point. For example, if a research question asks how new social media are affecting American politics, the corresponding thesis might argue that they change the role of youth in politics in three ways: by spurring political discussions, by recruiting young people to political events, and by influencing young people to vote. When identifying your thesis and supporting points, remember to maintain your sociological perspective (discussed in Chapter 1). Recall that sociology is about "people doing things together." Sociologists are interested in explaining differences among individuals, groups, and societies. Why do some people commit crimes but not others? Why are some organizations more open to new ideas than others? Why are some social groups on the average richer than others? Why are some societies monetarily richer than others? Many students revert to thinking about individual motivations, human nature, or common sense. Thinking sociologically also means *using* the concepts you have learned and viewing the world through them.

Prior to writing or after you have typed a draft, it is helpful to outline the main supporting points (see pp. 32–33). Below is an outline from the student sample paper by Mayank Chawla later in this chapter.

WHITE NOISE: COUNTRY MUSIC AND WHITE IDENTITY

I. Introduction
   a. Why the topic interests the author
   b. Sociological significance
II. Authenticity links music and identity: sense of family
III. Relationship to other genres and social groups, especially African Americans
IV. Place in rural white south: White patriarchy
   a. Conservative political connotations: white identity
   b. Subculture
V. Summary and conclusion

WRITING THE INTRODUCTION AND CONCLUSION FOR THE GENERAL RESEARCH PAPER

We have discussed the internal organization of the paper first because many people have difficulty writing the introduction and conclusion and they often postpone writing them. The introduction should grab the reader's attention and then encourage him or her to continue reading, while the conclusion should summarize the argument or text. Writers often begin their introduction with a fact or anecdote, as Mayank Chawla did in the following sample student paper; others make a general theoretical comment. One approach is to begin with an abstract idea and then narrow in on the topic. The standard format is that the introduction should present the research question, summarize the answer, and state why the thesis is important, incorporating the core sociological concepts being employed. Writing the paper like a novel and keeping the reader in suspense until the answer is revealed at the end should be used with great care and only after consulting with the instructor. In academic writing, clarity is more important than suspense, and withholding the main point can easily confuse the reader.

The conclusion recaps the main points, and while it may introduce new ideas, especially a paper's implications, the conclusion should not introduce new facts. The conclusion is also an appropriate place to state reservations, caveats, or shortcomings. This is where your ideas matter the most. Many writers find it helpful to write the conclusion after setting the paper aside for a few days to help them regain perspective.

Remember, no paper is perfect or complete. There are always limitations to studies performed, focuses that omit cases, exceptions to generalizations, and doubts about conclusions. Showing the reader that you are already aware of shortcomings demonstrates your level of sophistication.

A SAMPLE STUDENT PAPER

The following sample general research paper on country music was written by Mayank Chawla for an undergraduate course in sociology. She supports her thesis with information she obtained from library books, journal articles, and newspaper articles. Mayank's paper follows a variation of the three-part essay format as discussed in Chapter 1.

OUR COMMENTS

Mayank Chawla
Professor Roy

WHITE NOISE: COUNTRY MUSIC AND WHITE IDENTITY

The first thought that struck me was that it looked like Hitler's fantasy: a dozen happy, patriotic, rosy-cheeked, innocent, light-haired, blue-eyed, *white* children. At the least, I expected a token, light-skinned (most likely biracial) black girl (or two), sprinkled among the white kids. In the midst of public controversy over the lack of representation of people of color in the media, I recently saw a KZLA commercial that seemed suspiciously white and strategically patriotic, mentioning the word "American" multiple times in the advertisement. I dismissed my thought as racially hypersensitive, until I found other friends randomly pointing out the obvious whiteness of the advertisement.

Studies of race and music have exhaustively focused on people of color and their music in an institutionally racist society. In this paper, I invert the scholarly lens of observation to examine the presence of white identity in what we commonly hold as the quintessential music of white America: country music. Sociologically, historically, and politically, I explore how we have come to associate country music with whiteness, and the overall validity of this correlation. Most authors of extensive scholarly studies on country music are longtime country fans; their bias is reflected in a generally inadequate treatment of race and country music. Any mention of correlation between whiteness and country music is dismissed, justified, or minimized. In this paper, I argue that there exists a strong relationship between country music and whiteness. Although I am not personally a fan of country music, I do not seek to vilify the genre and its fans, but rather, to examine it as both a product and agent of white identity.

1

> Mayank opens with a personal observation but immediately connects it to sociological issues, telling us about the conventional wisdom in the literature and how she is adding to it. Her paper answers the question, "What exactly is the connection between country music and white identity?" Her paper answers this question by explaining how country music, which she argues is "for and by white people," expresses various social, political, and economic relationships.

This paragraph discusses too many topics, talking about authenticity, narrative, musical features of country music, the similarities to other genres, and its relationship to its audiences.

This paragraph expresses two ideas: it tells us about the audiences and about an exception to the music's white identity. The references to Charlie Pride, one of the few African American country music performers, would be better later in the paper, as a qualification to its main argument.

Masked behind a façade of "authenticity," country music, like all genres, is fabricated (Peterson 1997), making any essentialist characterization of country music difficult. However, a few general characteristics pervade all or most country music. A "storytellers medium," country songs have a strong sense of narratives, like mini, musical soap operas. The songs generally have simple chord structures, regular rhythm, and small melodic range. This simple musical structure highlights the narrative lyrics of country songs (Peterson and McLaurin 1992). Folk and pop songs, however, often possess the same elements, but do not fall within the genre of country music. Country music is not a genre defined by essential musical characteristics, but rather a reflection of the people and region from which it originated and the nation that consumes it.

"Participants in country music culture behave something like a vast extended family at an endless church supper in a rural American small town" (Ellison 1995:xvii). The audience is strikingly homogeneous: almost exclusively white, Christian, middle-aged, Republican, working class, and Southern (Danker 1991). The few blacks that enjoy country music generally grew up in the South. The performers are overwhelmingly white and 80% were born in the South (McLaurin 1992). Most of the country music studies I encountered are quick to mention Charlie Pride, the first and only successful black country singer. He came to the country music stage in 1961 and performed at the Grand Ole Opry in 1967 (Lawler 1996). As Barbara Ching points out, "Pride may well have suffered greatly from hard times, but the character he presents to the world is an unquestionably successful one who suffers no incurable unease" (Ching 2001:31). Pride's nonconfrontational demeanor allowed his incorporation into country music. He regularly ameliorated tension at his concerts by opening with some version of "I guess you're surprised to see me comin' out here wearin' this permanent tan and singing country music" (Ching 2001:31). Although Pride achieved moderate success in country music, no other black performer to date has achieved similar success. Pride himself once said, "I don't think of myself as the Jackie Robinson of country music . . . I'm just trying to be myself" (Lawler 1996:109). As a black man, Charlie Pride's break into the white genre was a unique exception, not the norm (Lawler 1996).

Paradoxically, country music, a supposedly authentically white genre, has its roots in African American musical forms. Bill C. Malone, the eminent country music scholar, argues that black or blackface musicians dominated music in the South, and it was not until later that rural white music gained prominence in the South (Malone 1993). Black and blackface minstrels had a profound influence on country music. Malone argues that minstrel songs, like "Old Zip Coon," "Away Down on the Old Plantation," and "Dixie" (Malone 1993) "lost their original 'Negro' connotations as they became part of the repertoire of country music" (Malone 2002). Prominent country singers like Jimmie Rodgers, Bob Wills, and Roy Acuff worked as blackface performers early in their careers (Tosches 1985); in 1953, the year before the landmark desegregation of public schools, the Grand Ole Opry's number-one tent show starred Jamup and Honey, two blackface performers (Malone 1993).

Blues and jazz, decidedly African American musical forms, have also had a penetrable influence on country music. Many major white country music performers were influenced and inspired by black blues and jazz musicians and their instruments. Richard A. Peterson, a prominent country music scholar, points out that although Jimmie Rodgers (Malone 1968) has a clearly white Southern twang, blues and jazz dominate in his music (Peterson 1997). The fiddle and the banjo, landmark instruments of rural white Southern music, were actually used by Southern blacks before being taken up by Southern whites (Malone 1968). In fact, white country performers have commonly used the phrase "nigger picking" to refer to the most complex guitar styles in country music (Malone 1968). As Malone (1968) points out, "[a]lthough Negro songs and styles have moved freely

> Offering an apparent paradox is an effective device for getting the reader's attention. Country music's strong roots in African American music are the kind of anomaly that begs for sociological explanation.

> The detailed examples of the artists and the titles of their songs are very effective; good writing is specific.

3

into white country music, Negroes have not" (p. 27). Paradoxically, black influence has been completely ignored in the "pure" white genre of country music, even by country artists who were inspired by black musicians. The Country Music Hall of Fame and Museum in Nashville fails to acknowledge any of the black performers who originated the style for which many early white country stars were famous (Peterson 1992). Country music has co-opted black musical forms and disseminated them as "purely white."

Connotations of country music as a white genre are not accidental. In *Creating Country Music: Fabricating Authenticity,* Peterson (1997) details the deliberate separation of white and black music in the South, as a strategic decision by record company executives. Industry competition led to segregated markets for country music. In the 1920's, Okey Record Company specifically marketed country music to poor whites. The opposite of "hillbilly music" was "race music," the wide range of music created by and marketed to blacks (Green 1965). Country music did not accidentally or coincidentally evolve into a white genre; it was deliberately crafted and institutionalized as an assertion of (rural) white identity.

Poor rural whites have historically suffered class oppression at the hands of upper middle-class whites. Because of this oppression, poor whites (including European immigrants) have repeatedly appealed to claims of whiteness to elevate their condition and avoid being equated with blacks. Eighteenth century rural songs, including "I'd rather be a nigger an' plow ol' Beack,/Dan a white hill-billy wid a long red neck" and "Oh poor olde hillbilly, oh, where do you stand,/while the Dark Tobacco Planters Association is forming its clan?" illustrate the fear of poor whites (Green 1965). This attitude continued into the twentieth century. The lyrics of Merle Haggard's song "I'm a White Boy," written in 1975, say "I'm proud and white. Daddy's name wasn't Willie Woodrow; I wasn't born in no ghetto" (Tosches 1985). After the Civil War, poor whites felt threatened by newfound black freedom (Peterson 1992). Minstrel shows, says whiteness

She tells us here who the actors were. The racial identity of country music did not just happen, but was the result of actions by specific people. But the transition into the paragraph could be smoother. The text jumps from a statement about how white record company executives shaped the music's identity to a discussion of the racial attitudes of poor rural white people.

Although Mayank has been careful with her citations, she forgets to include the page numbers for some of the quotes in this paragraph. Page numbers are needed so that a curious reader can find the quote.

4

scholar David Wellman (1997), "reassured white men who they were not: not black, not slave, not gay" (p. 312). Rural whites had a personal, social, and political interest in distancing themselves from blacks and identifying as white (Roediger 1994). Country music provided a vehicle for defending this interest. In asserting their whiteness, poor rural whites maintained a sense of working-class pride. Throughout time, country music has reflected white working-class woes. From sharecroppers to factory workers to truck drivers, country music has provided a venue of expression for poor white identity (Peterson 1991).

Country music originated in a region rooted in a rural economy and rural identity. The inherently conservative rural nature of country music protects white identity in the face of urban threats. Country music was constructed and marketed as a rural (white) music opposite urban (black) genres of blues and jazz. The rural nature of country music has adapted, retaining its increasing urbanization. Where rural people and cowboys once dominated the country music scene, truck drivers, or "eighteen-wheel cowboys" (Gregory 1989:242) epitomize the modern country music man. "Rural music did not die when it moved into the cities; it merely adapted itself to changed conditions." Rural settings symbolize "pure," wholesome white identity, while urban settings represent change, moral degeneration, and the infestation of nonwhites. In fact, Bruce Feiler wrote in a *New York Times* article, "[Country music] has become the de facto sound track of white flight" (Ware and Back 1992:266). In a nation moving towards urbanization, country music has glorified rural arrested development, and consequently, preservation of white purity (Malone 1968).

Country music represents the ideology of the white South—an ideology rooted in slavery and segregation. Southern pride continues to be a strong force in country music. For example, "most country music continues to be produced in Nashville, the capital city of a former Confederate state" (McLaurin 1992:24). Country songs throughout time repeatedly allude to a

When Mayank quotes journalist Bruce Feiler, she explains that he wrote in the *New York Times.* This identification could be critical for the reader to understand the quotation because the *New York Times* is a national newspaper and reflects a journalist's opinion for a national audience.

5

sense of place, often mentioning names of specific Southern towns, cities, and states. Historian Tom Connelly calls country music "The great modern expression of the Lost Cause mentality" (McLaurin 1992:15). "Lost Cause mentality" implies that white Southerners have an inferiority complex, due to the defeat of the Confederate army, and continue to hold a renewed sense of pride in the (Confederate) South. Country music is, hence, a manifestation of this renewed white Southern pride.

Paradoxically, country music is intensely patriotic, given that Southerners once wanted to secede from the Union (McLaurin 1992). In fact, Southern pride in the courage of Confederate fighters lends itself well to a virulent American patriotism (McLaurin 1992). The dualism inherent in country music has easily translated into pro-American sentiment. In repeatedly presenting itself as the quintessential American genre, country music is antiforeign. During World War II, a good number of patriotic country songs contained a "get the dirty little Jap" type of racism. Similarly, in the era of McCarthy and the Cold War, patriotic, anticommie songs were popular, including, "They Locked God Outside the Iron Curtain," "The Red That We Want is the Red We've Got in the Old Red, White, and Blue," and "Korea, Here We Come" (DiMaggio, Peterson, and Esco 1972:45). The strongly antiforeign, patriotic nature of country music reflects poor whites' desires to enter mainstream white American society. As McLaurin notes, "Since the Civil War and Reconstruction, Southerners have struggled to remove the stigma and prove themselves truly loyal Americans" (McLaurin 1992:28).

White patriarchy is a central focus of country music. Country music constructs white masculinity as the "gendered and racialized obligation to paternal protection of the white family" (Lipsitz 1998:75). Implicit in Southern notions of white masculinity is an obsession with the protection of white womanhood. Historically, white Southerners have viewed white women as innocent and vulnerable to the predatory tendencies of black

---

[Margin note 1] Here she is elaborating on the theme introduced earlier that country music grew out of Southern white culture.

[Margin note 2] Like much recent sociological writing, here she is introducing gender dynamics to complement the analysis of race; however, this paragraph is too brief to be convincing. She offers keen insight but needs more evidence. Note how Mayank provides a smooth transition from the end of this paragraph to the beginning of the next paragraph, echoing the concepts in each.

men. Masculine obligation to the family is not simply a personal, but a *racial* obligation. As a product of a region where white womanhood is sanctified, country music is racially patriarchal.

Epitomized as a "pure" and "authentic" white form, country music has been widely used by white supremacist groups. A well-distributed 1925 poster of famous fiddler John Carson shows Carson standing in front of a KKK sign, at the Mountain City, Tennessee Old Time Fiddling Contest, sponsored by the KKK (Peterson 1997). During the Korean War, white supremacist groups distributed underground racist country recordings, like "Move Them Niggers North," "Kajun Klu Klux Klan," and "Nigger, Nigger," by the Coon Hunters, which talked about tarring and feathering Martin Luther King Jr. (Malone 1968). Some of these recordings were sold over the counter at an Atlanta F. W. Woolworth until 1967 (Peterson 1992). The appeal of country music to white supremacist groups was due to the national image of country as an authentic, purely white genre.

The "pure" white image of country music developed as the nation became interested in finding and reclaiming a pure, untainted white male identity. This search for an authentic white identity propagated the "widely shared belief that the Appalachia preserved the nation's genes, culture, and values of the original white settlers" (Campbell 1999). The nation was obsessed with recovering untainted "Anglo-Saxon" roots and the Appalachia seemed like a treasure-chest. There was a widely-held belief that the West was America's last frontier. This fear of the vanishing frontier coincided with a fear of the feminization and weakening of the pure, rugged, individualistic white man (Slotkin 1992). Hence, began the nation's glorification of the American cowboy.

Rugged, courageous, violent, and white, the singing cowboy became an American idol and sex symbol. Hollywood played a crucial role in the romanticization of America's cowboy past and the national popularization of country music (Malone 1968). America's most famous singing cowboy,

7

Gene Autry, symbolized white America's obsession with reclaiming what it perceived as vanishing white male hegemony and red-blooded Americanism (Horsman 1997). As Gavin James Campbell notes in his dissertation, "The perceived loss of mastery over African Americans, women, lower-class whites, and the fear that urban life had feminized white men to the point of helplessness . . . made both the mountaineer and the old-time fiddler more attractive than ever" (Campbell 1999). Nineteenth-century complications of race-relations propagated the nation's nostalgia for simpler times in a "racially-pure mountain South in which blacks simply vanished" (Campbell 1999). The theme of "ethnic pluralism" in the 1960's gave whites further permission to glorify and romanticize our white Western cowboy past (Gregory 1989). Country singers gladly accepted and played into stereotypes of the rugged singing cowboy (Malone 1993).

Country music's current conservative, right-wing leanings are ironic, given the initial populist leanings of the genre (Malone 2002). The "hillbilly" was once the white counterpart of the black "sambo" (Peterson 1992). The development of a distinct poor white culture was in fact prompted by marginalization. Shunned by mainstream white society, poor Southern whites clustered in neighborhoods and developed and maintained a distinct identity and culture (McLaurin 1992). With its strongly conservative leanings, country music continued to express the concerns of the urban white working man through the 1970's and 1980's. Johnny Paycheck's "Take This Job and Shove It!" gained popularity in the early 1970's, while Dolly Parton's "9 to 5" described working class concerns of the 1980's. Today, a major theme in country music is the working truck driver (Peterson 1992).

Country music swung toward the right when folk music broke away from the genre. Country music, as the music of the "common man," was at some point used by left-wing radicals and reformers to challenge capitalism (Malone 1968). Consequently, urban folk music broke off from country

> Having discussed race and gender, the paper now addresses class. Many readers would have appreciated a signpost that showed the order and movement of major ideas in her outline. A clear signal phrase or transitional sentence would have helped the reader understand that the paper is now turning to the issue of class.

music. While country music is inherently conservative and sought to preserve the status quo, folk music advocated change and criticized the status quo. As Jennifer Lawler astutely points out, "folk and country had the same heritage . . . the split was political." While the music remained similar the message was radically different, to the point where "soon fans of one could not very easily be fans of the other" (Lawler 1996:23). Folk music has a strong protest element, while antiprotest themes pervade country music. While folk represented left-wing progressives, country came to represent right-wing conservatives.

From the 1960's, country music and the neo-conservative right-wing had a mutually reinforcing relationship. Right-wing politicians adopted country music for political ends, and country artists willingly catered to the right-wing to bolster their popularity. Gregory interestingly notes, "northern blue-collar constituencies which thirty years before had been at the very heart of New Deal liberalism were changing political coloration . . . Threatened by the civil rights agenda of liberal democrats . . . they were moving towards a politics of racial and patriotic conservatism" (Gregory 1989:242). Racist Alabama governor George Wallace adopted country music to the point where every Wallace rally incorporated country music (Malone 2002). Wallace's overwhelming appeal to the country music community reflects the genre's interest in protecting white privilege. Threatened by the counterculture of the 1960's, right-wing politicians gained an even broader conservative following by the 1970's. Richard Nixon called Merle Haggard's conservative song, "Okie from Muskogee," the "true voice of the silent American majority" (McLaurin 1992). Jimmy Carter publicly showed an affinity for country. Both Ronald Reagan and George H. W. Bush used Lee Greenwood's popular "God Bless the U.S.A." in their second presidential campaigns (Ellison 1995). In the late 1980's, George H. W. Bush proclaimed country music to be his favorite (Malone 2002). In fact, Naomi Judd and Tanya Tucker performed at the Republican

9

> Mayank's paper is well organized. The beginning of almost every paragraph tracks a new main idea that is developed with explanations and examples.

> Note the use of ellipses (. . .) to indicate that one or more words are deleted from a quotation.

> Stating that Democrat Jimmy Carter also liked country music weakens Mayank's point that country music has appealed to conservative political leaders.

convention where Bush was nominated. Late in the campaign, Bush sprinkled campaign speeches with phrases from country song lyrics.

The new right's objective was to dismantle political gains of the Civil Rights movement. Since it could not explicitly reverse these gains, it had to rearticulate their goals in the context of asserting a positive white identity and wholesome American values, like "defense of traditional values, opposition to 'big government' and patriotic, [religious] and militaristic themes" (Omi and Winant 1944:124). The close relationship between a neoconservative agenda and the country music community, although paradoxical, is not difficult to see. The values that the new right defended aligned almost perfectly with the country music community, and both groups had a strong interest in reinforcing the existing racial hierarchy. As Malone (1998) suggests, "the national mood of conservatism may have inspired a rediscovery of the mythic South as a region of contentment, stability, and bucolic values" (p. 117).

Although country music reinforces white identity, it manages to do so without explicit references to white racial identity. Ironically, in a genre shaped by race relations, explicit mentions of race are virtually absent in country music. Country music is not called "white" music, but it is called purely and authentically "American." As Richard Dyer astutely notes, "White power secures its dominance by seeming not to be anything in particular" (Lipsitz, 1998:1). Transparency is a key component of white power. Transparency allows white identity to be neutral, universal identity, when it is really white identity. However, "the assumption that white people are just people, which is not far off from saying that white people are people whereas other colors are something else" (Dyer 1997:2). Country music's assertion of *white* American identity is unnecessarily redundant, since "American" is generally short for "white American." The assertion of a white identity can be problematic, even in the midst of ethnic pluralism. Ian Haney-Lopez (1992) explains that "celebrating whiteness even with the

One of the challenges of interpretive analysis is explaining how a cultural form implies a meaning even though there is no explicit reference. For example, Mayank makes a case that country music expresses a white identity even though it never mentions whiteness. This is the conclusion her paper has been leading to, so the discussion is becoming more abstract, relating to the broader social dynamics of how race works. And here she clearly presents her opinion.

10

best of antiracist intentions, seems likely only to entrench the status quo of racial beliefs" (p. 72). Country music, as a symbol of an authentic white America, has troubling implications for our nation's future.

Once the "language of a subculture" (Gregory 1989), country music has penetrated the mainstream. The proliferation of country artists in popular American culture continues to intensify. Country performers, like LeAnn Rimes, Shania Twain, and Faith Hill have had enormous success crossing over into popular music, while retaining loyal country followers. Country music has transformed from the music of "plainfolk Americanism" (Gregory 1989) into the music of mainstream materialism. The positive aspect of the mainstreaming of country music is that it brings a more diverse audience to the genre. The aforementioned artists have a larger proportion of nonwhite fans than artists before them. Played repeatedly on mainstream popular radio stations, people of color have been exposed and warmed up to country music. The negative facet of country mainstreaming is that it popularizes a genre, reinforcing white identity. "In the video age, country and western has become the last oasis of white American values" (Ware and Back 1992:266). Country mainstreaming may imply the further mainstreaming of white identity.

Despite the strong correlation between country music and whiteness, several popular country music artists have been able to criticize and push the boundaries of the genre. Johnny Cash, who has recorded over a thousand country songs since 1955, has publicly defended the rights of convicts, Native Americans, illiterate people, and people of color. To show his identification with marginalized people, Cash almost always appeared wearing black (Danker 1992). In his song, "Man in Black," he says he "will wear black until the world is in better shape and he can wear colors" (Lawler 1996:140). Cash's popular "Six White Horses" describes his grief over the killings of Jesus, the Kennedy brothers, and Martin Luther King Jr. (DiMaggio, Peterson, and Esco 1972). Lawler (1996) points out that he "managed to appeal to the rugged individualism dear to the country music fan's heart, as well as maintain a sense of justice and compassion that led him to protest many conditions and situations in America" (p. 140).

Garth Brooks, one of the most popular modern country performers, has spoken explicitly about the environment, domestic violence, famine, civil rights, date rape, and lesbian, gay, bisexual, and transgender (LGBT) issues. He has managed to redefine conservative country music ideology, without abandoning the country community. He once said,

> I think the Republicans' big problem is that they believe family values are June and Walt and 2.3 children. To me it means laughing, being able to dream . . . if a set of parents are black and white, or two people of the same sex, or if one man or one woman acts as the parents, that the children grow up happy and healthy: that's what family values are. (Ellison 1995:259)

The statement sums up Brooks's challenge to traditional, white, patriarchal, and heterosexist country music values. He has managed to extend the boundaries of country music, without abandoning the genre all together.

Finally, k. d. lang, the first publicly lesbian country music star, poses the largest challenge to country music. Although she has not been widely accepted by conventional country fans, her presence and in-your-face image force country music to confront and question its conservative nature. She challenged country music ideas about white female performers in the genre. Lang has, in fact, acknowledged that country music is a white genre that alienated many people of color. Rather than being a puppet to the country music community, lang has redefined country music. For example, she once taped a PETA promotional spot saying, "meat stinks, and if you knew how meat was made, you'd probably lose your lunch," to the chagrin of country fans in cattle country. Although she directly challenged the conservative nature of country music, her confrontational

"Finally" is a helpful signpost to the end of a list. Mayank uses many transitional expressions throughout her paper, for example, "consequently," "however," "in fact."

12

approach has alienated the traditional country music audience (Lawler 1996:69–70).

Country music is white noise, literally. In this paper, I have outlined the social, political, and economic relationship between country music and white identity. Country music is music for and by white people. Massive societal upheaval and progress in the past century have been unable to penetrate country music, keeping the genre, its performers, and its audience exclusively white. Country music is white noise, figuratively. Whiteness is omnipresent, but never explicit, in country music. It remains in the background, presenting itself as a race-free form, when it, in fact, reinforces white pride and existing racial hierarchies. As I stated earlier, I do not seek to vilify country music, nor do I advocate the complete annihilation of the genre. Rather, I encourage critical dialogue about country music's relationship to race, in hopes that further understanding will shape and open the future course of country music into a genre that truly represents the American people.

> She finishes with a summary, restating her main points.

REFERENCES

Campbell, Gavin James. 1999. *Music and the Making of a Jim Crow Culture, 1900–1925*. Chapel Hill: University of North Carolina at Chapel Hill.

Ching, Barbara. 2001. *Wrong's What I Do Best: Hard Country Music and Contemporary Culture*. New York: Oxford University Press.

Danker, Frederick E. 1992. "The World According to Johnny Cash: Lyrical Themes in His Music." Pp. 131–154 in *You Wrote My Life: Lyrical Themes in Country Music*, edited by Melton A. McLaurin and Richard A. Peterson. Philadelphia: Gordon and Breach Science Publishers.

DiMaggio, Paul, Richard A. Peterson, and Jack Esco, Jr. 1972. "Country Music: Ballad of the Silent Majority." Pp. 38–55 in *The Sounds of Social Change: Studies in Popular Culture*, edited by R. Serge Denisoff and Richard A. Peterson. Chicago: Rand McNally & Co.

> In her original paper, Mayank prints the Reference section on a new page. Following the guidelines in Chapter 5 she places the heading at the left-hand margin, types it in all capital letters, and triple-spaces between the heading and the first source listed. According to the *ASA Style Guide* (2010), with the exception of New York, both the city and state of the publisher should be included.

13

Dryer, Richard. 1997. "The Matter of Whiteness." Pp. 1–40 in *White*. New York: Routledge.

Ellison, Curtis W. 1995. *Country Music Culture: From Hard Times to Heaven*. Jackson: University Press of Mississippi.

Foley, Neil. 1997. *The White Scourge: Mexicans, Blacks, and Poor Whites in Texas Cotton Culture*. CA: University of California Press.

Green, Archie. 1965. "Hillbilly Music: Source and Symbol." *Journal of American Folklore* 78:204–28.

Gregory, James N. 1989. *American Exodus: The Dust Bowl Migration and Okie Culture in California*. New York: Oxford University Press.

Haney-Lopez, Ian. 1992. "White Race Consciousness." Pp. 155–195 in *White by Law: The Legal Construction of Race,* edited by Ian Haney Lopez. New York: New York University Press.

Horsman, Reginald. 1997. "Race and Manifest Destiny: The Origins of American Racial Anglo-Saxonism." Pp. 139–44 in *Critical White Studies: Looking Behind the Mirror,* edited by Richard Delgado and Jean Stefancie. Philadelphia: Temple University Press.

Lawler, Jennifer. 1996. *Songs of Life: The Meaning of Country Music*. Kansas: Pogo Press.

Lipsitz, George. 1998. *The Possessive Investment in Whiteness: How White People Profit From Identity Politics*. Philadelphia: Temple University Press.

Malone, Bill C. 1968. *Country Music U.S.A.* Austin: University of Texas Press.

Malone, Bill C. 2002. *Don't Get Above Your Raisin': Country Music and Southern Working Class*. Chicago: University of Illinois Press.

Malone, Bill C. 1998. "The Rural South Moves to the City: Country Music Since World War II." Pp. 95–121 in *The Rural South Since World War II*, edited by R. Douglas Hurt. Louisiana: Louisiana State University Press.

Malone, Bill C. 1993. *Singing Cowboys and Musical Mountaineers: Southern Culture and the Roots of Country Music*. Athens: University of Georgia Press.

[Note: To save space, only half of Mayank's references are reproduced here.]

Here Mayank includes the state but not the city of the source. Both the city and the state of the source should be included.

Both the volume number and the issue number should be included in the References for a journal article.

14

C H A P T E R
E I G H T

The Quantitative Research Paper

In a quantitative research paper, numerical data are collected to answer a sociological question. Because quantitative research depends on specific techniques of data collection and analysis, this chapter (unlike the previous two chapters) may be most useful to students who have taken or are taking an introductory research methods course or an elementary statistics course.

Quantitative methods are more formalized than other methods. Papers based on quantitative methods generally follow a specific format, the journal format (see Chapter 2 "Developing an Argument: Logic and Structure"), and are divided into four major sections. Students sometimes find the clear definition of format makes writing easier because they don't have to worry about how to organize their paper.

Briefly, the issues that should be covered in each section of a quantitative research paper include:

1. **Literature Review.** After a review of the relevant theory and literature, what sociological question do you feel needs to be addressed? What, if any, expectations (hypotheses) do you have about the answer?
2. **Methods.** The method section is generally divided into three subsections:
   Sample. How did you select your sample?

Measures. What measures did you use?
Procedure. What method did you use in trying to answer your question?
3. **Results.** What patterns of numerical data did you find?
4. **Discussion.** Do the data support or fail to support your hypotheses? What do your data mean? How do they relate to theory and/or previous empirical research?

Although the length of the four major sections is about equal for published papers using sophisticated methods and analyses, the introduction and discussion sections for student papers are generally slightly longer than the other two sections. However, the relative length of the sections will depend on the amount of detail required by your instructor for describing your methods and results. In addition to these major sections, other important components of your paper include the title, abstract, references, and appendix.

Since journal styles vary, ask your instructor which professional or scholarly journal format you should use. For example, the advice given in this chapter is based on the fourth edition of the *American Sociological Association Style Guide* (2010). It may be sufficient to simply follow the style used by the journal your instructor recommends. Before starting your paper, examine recent articles from the recommended journal or, if none is recommended, use the *American Sociological Review*, the top-tier journal published by the American Sociological Association (ASA). Download to a storage device, e-mail, or photocopy one or two sample journal articles to use as a model of format and tone. Your paper should not only look professional but sound professional as well. Scientific communication uses a formal prose style.

We have arranged the topics covered in this chapter according to the steps you should follow in writing your quantitative research paper. For example, although the title and the abstract are placed at the beginning of your paper, you should write them during the final stages so that they describe your entire study. Therefore, we cover these components toward the end of the chapter.

WRITING AN INTRODUCTION

The first step in preparing a quantitative paper is to write an introduction, even before collecting your data or selecting your method. The introduction will guide your research and help determine your focus. The purpose of the introduction is to provide a context for formulating and operationalizing your research questions or hypotheses. Writing an introduction involves searching and reviewing the literature, stating the problem and framing a sociological research question, and where appropriate developing hypotheses.

REVIEWING THE LITERATURE AND WRITING YOUR LITERATURE REVIEW

Once you decide on a topic, use the reference sources listed in Chapter 4 to search for similar empirical studies of the topic. Also gather books and articles on the theory you plan to use as a framework for your study. Read and take notes as you would for a textual analysis paper (see Chapter 6).

The purpose of reviewing the literature is not simply to find out what has been done on your topic but to determine what has been *done well*. Rather than accept the existing research at face value, students writing a quantitative research paper are trying to develop a justification for doing additional research. To accomplish this, a student needs to find a weakness in the logic and/or methods of previous studies. Alternatively, a student might look for gaps in what is known. After reviewing what has been done, it should become evident what has *not* been done or what has not been done *well*. By finding an area of research that has not been adequately studied or one that has been understudied, you will be able to justify new data collection and make a contribution to the literature.

In writing your literature review, provide enough background material to contextualize the formulation of your research questions or hypotheses. Begin your review with a summary of the theory or theories from which your questions are derived, specifying their major tenets and focusing on one or two major concepts to be tested. Next, discuss each relevant study, summarizing in a few sentences the theoretical approach, major research questions or hypotheses, operational definitions (that is, how the variables studied were measured), and conclusions drawn in each study. It is often helpful to arrange the studies in chronological order. How do these studies fit together? Do they form a pattern or are they inconsistent? Do they fail to account for an important variable? What direction do they suggest for future research?

STATING THE PROBLEM AND FORMULATING RESEARCH QUESTIONS

The statement of the problem reveals the gaps or contradictory findings that you found after reviewing the relevant theory and literature. Its purpose is to move beyond previous studies and highlight theoretical inconsistencies in need of resolution, methodological problems apparent in the empirical literature, and/or the logical next step that research in this area should take. For example, you may want to concentrate on a different interpretation of a theory not adequately tested; set up a critical test of two rival theories; extend the theory to a new population or substantive area; use a new operational definition of a concept; correct the faulty methodology of a previous study; use a different design or method; or include more variables in order to look for possible interactions. For some class assignments a simple replication of a published study may be sufficient. Be sure to check with your instructor. However, unless your study is an exact replication of an earlier study, you must explain how your study differs from previous works, how your study will extend their findings, and what your study will contribute.

Following from the literature review, the statement of the problem should suggest research questions that need to be answered—for example, "To what extent do people with more education get high-status jobs than people with less education?" Sometimes the theory or literature reviewed can provide expected answers to these questions. When they do, the questions can be refined and developed into hypotheses—for example, "If ethnicity is held constant, an increase in education will be associated with an increase in occupational attainment." A hypothesis is a formal statement about the relationship you expect to find between two or more concepts (see below). However, sometimes theory or previous literature does not provide enough information to allow someone to make an educated guess about the answer to a research question. When this is the case, these can be left as research questions to be answered by the paper. Most quantitative papers examine more than one hypothesis or research question.

STATING YOUR HYPOTHESES

Your literature review and statement of the problem show the logic that led to the development of your hypotheses. They serve as a sort of preliminary evidence. If your reasoning is sound, the numerical data you collect will provide further support for each of your hypotheses.

Each hypothesis should be stated in such a way that it can be unambiguously confirmed or rejected by the results. That is, you should be able to state "If the data show this, then we can conclude the hypothesis is supported; however, if the data show otherwise, we will conclude the hypothesis is not supported." Additionally, each hypothesis should be stated in such a way as to make clear the type (causal or correlational) and direction (positive or negative) of the expected relationships. That is, does any particular hypothesis postulate that one variable causes the other, or does it simply state that the two variables are correlated? If the relationship between the variables is believed to be causal, which is the independent variable (the variable that causes or leads to another variable) and which is the dependent variable (the variable that is the effect or the outcome of another variable)? If the relationship is believed to be correlational rather than causal, are the variables expected to be related positively (as X increases, Y increases) or negatively (as X increases, Y decreases)? Note, in correlational studies where there is no assumption about the causal order of the variables, no distinction is made between the independent and dependent variables.

In stating your hypothesis it is important to explain how the variables will be operationally defined, that is, the manner in which the variables will be measured. Your operational definition of variables should include your unit of analysis, for example, individuals, groups, institutions, or countries.

DEVELOPING A METHODS AND ANALYSIS PLAN

Once you have drafted your literature review and stated your research questions or hypotheses, you are ready to proceed with the development of a methods and analysis plan. Conducting a sound investigation is crucial to writing a good quantitative research paper. Therefore, it is necessary to consider in advance all the decisions you must make in collecting your data. Drawing up a methods and analysis plan will greatly improve the quality of your paper and will make the writing process go more smoothly. Although it is beyond the scope of this book to discuss the multitude of methodological and statistical factors that need to be considered in conducting a good quantitative study, we do address those issues important to writing a good report of your study.

You will be limited to certain methods depending on the hypothesis you are testing or the kind of research question you are trying to answer. For example, if you are interested in the mortality (death) rates of upper- versus lower-class men, you would have to use archival sources rather than a survey. The most common methods used to collect quantitative data are archival sources, structured observation, experiment, and survey.

Archival sources are records of preexisting data. Examples of archival sources are censuses, books, magazines, newspapers, photographs, and other artifacts of a cultural group. Although census data is obtained from surveys, we include them as archival because the results are stored in electronic archives or published in tables available in government documents and books. The U.S. Census Bureau conducts a complete census of the American population every 10 years as well as many smaller studies. As noted in Chapter 4, extensive amounts of data are available at http://www.census.gov. Published census data consist of official records of information including rates of birth, death, marriage, divorce, crime, suicide, and accidents.

Structured observation can be conducted in a laboratory or in the "field" (real-world settings). Structured field observation, unlike ethnographic field research discussed in the next chapter, is guided by set hypotheses or specific measurement objectives. With structured observation, you need to know in advance what variables you plan to observe. Whether it is done in a laboratory or in the field, structured observation can often involve simple counting, such as counting the occurrence of certain behaviors or counting the number of people in different situations. For instance, you may want to observe the frequency with which men as compared with women make supportive statements during group discussions, or count the number of students who attend political rallies on campus versus off campus. People's behavior online can also be studied using structured observation. Software programs can capture or scrape Web activities in social media such as blogs, Twitter, or Facebook. Sociologists are just beginning to develop observational methods for collecting data in this way.

There are many different *experimental* designs, but the basic model involves two groups—an experimental group and a control group. Both groups are treated exactly the same except for the independent variable(s), which is (are) manipulated. Although we usually think of experiments as conducted in a laboratory, experiments can also be conducted in everyday settings (called "field experiments"). For example, suppose a researcher wants to examine whether people in a shopping mall are more likely to come to the aid of a well-dressed victim or a shabbily dressed victim. They could create an experiment where a confederate (or accomplice of the researcher) alternates wearing a suit with wearing dirty jeans and a torn T-shirt when asking shoppers for help. The researcher could then evaluate the shoppers' willingness to help, and if it changes, depending on what the confederate is wearing.

The *survey* method includes both questionnaires and interviews. The logic of the survey is to replicate the experimental method artificially without the same degree of control, by comparing two or more groups of survey respondents or interview subjects. The groups can be based on response scores (for example, those who score high or low on a particular attitude measure) or on demographic characteristics (for example, Catholics and Protestants, blacks and whites, young and old, or high and low socioeconomic status). In a survey, unlike an experiment, the independent variable is not manipulated. Instead, the researcher focuses on response differences that result from the naturally existing differences in the respondents. For example, if you are interested in the different responses of males and females to a series of questions, your independent variable would be gender of respondent.

For census statistics about the United States, an excellent government publication available in most college and university libraries or online is the Historical Statistics of the United States (hsus.cambridge.org), which must be accessed through a university network or with a university proxy. A portal to a broad variety of federal government statistics is http://www.census.gov/compendia/statab/guide_to_sources.html.

When you analyze survey data collected by other researchers, it is called secondary data analysis. There are many major surveys that are now available from which professional sociologists and students alike can do simple analyses of survey results or download raw data for analysis. The Interuniversity Consortium for Political and Social Research (ICPSR) Web site (http://www.icpsr.umich.edu/icpsrweb/ICPSR/) offers the most extensive digital social science collection of databases; it includes data from thousands of studies that are available for public access. The General Social Survey discussed in Chapter 4 is one commonly used dataset that is included in ICPSR. The ASA also has a list of Public Data Resources for Sociologists online at http://www2.asanet.org/student/pubdata00a.html.

Whichever type of method you choose, be sure that your proposed research is in line with the guidelines set forth by the Institutional Review Board or Office for the Protection of Human Subjects on your campus (ask your instructor for details). You may need to get approval for your project from this committee before you collect your data.

Once you have decided on a method, draw up a plan for data collection and analysis to show your instructor. A methods and analysis plan ensures, *before you collect the data*, that your study will actually provide a test of your hypotheses. Further, it guarantees that you will be able to make sense of your data and analyze them successfully. Many students waste time and effort collecting large amounts of data only to discover later that the data do not provide a test of their hypotheses. Or, they find that they don't know how to go about analyzing the data. A methods and analysis plan can prevent these problems. Below we list the issues you should address in your methods and analysis plan.

QUESTIONS TO ADDRESS IN DEVELOPING YOUR METHODS AND ANALYSIS PLAN

1. What population will you sample? How will you select your sample? If you are conducting a field study, either a structured field observation or field experiment, what setting will you choose? Do you anticipate any problems in gaining access to the respondents or the field setting? How many observations will you need to make? With the exception of an archival study, no matter which type of method you decide to use to collect your data, you need to specify how many respondents (of each type) you will need to question or observe. Describe relevant characteristics of the sample, such as the number of respondents of each age, race/ethnicity, class, and gender.

If you are doing an archival study, documents, rather than people, constitute your sample. For example, in the sample student paper at the end of this chapter, the sample is magazine advertisements. Just as with human samples, you must describe the important characteristics of your archival sample. Shannon's sample included advertisements in women's magazines targeted to three different race/ethnic groups (African American, Hispanic, and white).

2. What measures will you use? That is, how will you operationalize your variables? (To operationalize your variables means to define the specific operations, methods, or procedures you will use to measure your variables.) If you are designing an interview or questionnaire, what question(s) will you ask to measure each concept? For example, if one of the concepts you are interested in is traditional gender-role attitudes, you might operationally define this as an affirmative answer (either "strongly agree" or "agree") to the statement "It goes against nature to place women in positions of authority over men." On the other hand, liberal gender-role attitudes would be operationally defined as a negative answer (either "strongly disagree" or "disagree") to the same statement.

How long will the questionnaire or survey take to answer? If you plan on conducting an interview or survey, will you use closed-ended questions, also known as "fixed-response," or open-ended questions? What will be the possible range of the response scale for the closed-ended questions? For example, a Likert Scale gives a continuum of possible answers to a statement or question, e.g., "Strongly disagree," "Disagree," "Neutral," "Agree," and "Strongly Agree."

If you plan to do a structured observation, whether it is in a field or laboratory setting, what exactly will you look for? How long should each observation last? What things will you want to have on your observation checklist (the list of things that you intend to count or measure)? For example, if you want to observe differences in how near people of different cultures tend to stand to one another, you might want to have a checklist that includes several different races/ethnicities and distances.

If you plan to conduct an archival study, you will need to find out the types of data that are available to you. Further, you will need to determine the form in which these data are presented. For example, if you are interested in comparing the birthrates of different religious groups, you will need to find out if the birthrates presented in the census tables are broken down by religious affiliation.

If you plan to conduct an interview or survey, you will need to develop a questionnaire (or survey instrument). Even when conducting an experiment in the laboratory or in the field, you generally will want to interview respondents or have them complete a questionnaire at the conclusion of the experiment. Although it is beyond the scope of this book to discuss all the details of creating a sound instrument, there are general guidelines that you should consider in order to facilitate the writing of your report. Instructors often expect you to include a copy of your instrument in the appendix of your paper. It is best to include your instrument in your methods and analysis plan and to have it approved by your instructor before you collect your data.

In developing your measures, it is best to begin by looking at those developed by other researchers. Scales exist that have already been shown to be valid and reliable. Many of these scales are reproduced at the end of journal articles or in books on measurement such as the *Handbook of Multicultural Measures* (2010) by Gamst, Liang, and Der-Karabetian published by Sage

Publications, Thousand Oaks, California. If you use an existing scale, be sure to refer to the name of the scale and its originator in the body of your paper (for example, "Rosenberg's Self-Esteem Scale was administered to respondents.") and to include the source of the scale in your list of references.

However, you might consider constructing some original questions to use in conjunction with an existing scale or modifying existing questions to better suit the purpose of your study. The following guidelines should be helpful if you decide to construct your own questions.

Guidelines for Questionnaire Construction

- Avoid using ambiguous terms or slang. Define the terms you use. For example, in the questionnaire on student dating shown in Figure 8–1, the term "date" is defined in question #7. Since dating patterns have changed over the years, there might have been some confusion as to what was meant by this term had this point not been clarified.
- Avoid "double-barreled" questions. Questions that contain "and" or "or" (such as "Do you feel that physical attractiveness or attitude similarity are important characteristics in a dating partner?") make it impossible to know whether the respondent views one or both characteristics as important.
- Avoid biased questions that lead the respondent to answer in a socially desirable way. For example, rather than asking, "Have you ever had a date?" You might ask the question, "Have you dated in the last year?" Respondents may be reluctant to say that they have never dated. However, they may feel comfortable saying they have not dated recently.
- If it is not necessary to know your respondent's name, don't ask for it. Anonymous questionnaires, that is, those that don't ask for a respondent's name, are more likely to yield honest answers.
- Provide adequate instructions about how to answer the questions. For example, the instructions "rate how important each date characteristic is to you" let respondents know they are being asked for their own opinion, not the opinion they believe to be held by their peer group.
- Number each question in the questionnaire. Space questions out on the page so they are easy to read.
- Be careful about the order in which questions are listed. Put easy questions first and difficult or sensitive questions last.
- Show respect for your respondents. Thank them for their cooperation and retain the confidentiality of their responses; do not reveal any information that could be used to identify them.

Alternatively, your assignment may allow you to use not only existing measures developed by other researchers, but their data as well. If secondary data analysis is acceptable for the purposes of your assignment, your task for the methods and analysis plan would involve the selection of an appropriate database, and, within that, the selection of specific questions to be used in your analysis.

FIGURE 8–1

EXAMPLE OF A QUESTIONNAIRE

Questionnaire # _____

Student Dating Questionnaire

The following questionnaire is anonymous. Your answers will be held in the strictest confidence.

Please circle your answers to the following questions.

1. What is your gender?
    a. male
    b. female

Using the five-point scale (where 1 = not at all important and 5 = extremely important), please rate how important each characteristic is *to you* in a dating partner.

		Not at All Important				Extremely Important
2.	Physical Attractiveness	1	2	3	4	5
3.	Personality	1	2	3	4	5
4.	Sense of Humor	1	2	3	4	5
5.	Potential Occupational Success	1	2	3	4	5
6.	Attitude Similarity	1	2	3	4	5

7. Have you dated in the last year (that is, gone out with someone of the opposite sex, or of the same sex, for purely social purposes with the possibility of developing a romantic involvement)?
    a. yes
    b. no

8. What is your sexual orientation?
    a. heterosexual
    b. homosexual
    c. bisexual
    d. prefer not to answer

Thank you for taking the time to complete this questionnaire. Your cooperation is greatly appreciated!

3. How will you get the data into an analyzable form? For example, have you assigned an appropriate numerical equivalent (low = 1, high = 2) to each of the response categories of closed-ended questions? Have you developed a coding scheme for open-ended questions? Your coding scheme could involve counting the number of respondents who made a reference to social mobility in response to an open-ended question, or counting the number of times different types of respondents mentioned themes of alienation. Remember that in a quantitative paper, you must be able to represent all responses numerically.

If you are an advanced student planning on forming an attitude index, or scale, from a set of closed-ended questions, will the response scores of any of your questions need to be reversed? That is, before adding together the response scores of several questions to form a single scale, will the response scores of negatively worded questions be reversed to correspond with the positively worded questions? Will you leave the index as a continuous variable or will you divide it at the median so as to compare high and low scorers?

4. How will you analyze the data? Depending on your hypotheses and the level of statistical knowledge required for your assignment, there are different options available for analyzing the data. If you have not taken a statistics course, the two simplest ways to analyze your data would be to calculate the percentages of or averages on each variable, independent of other variables. Independent percentages or averages are adequate for reporting the results of a descriptive study.

However, in testing hypotheses it is usually necessary to look at the relationship between two variables. The complexity of calculating averages or percentages increases when you examine the relationship between two variables, because the variables must be examined jointly. Some common methods of doing this include constructing a table of means (see Figure 8–2), a cross-tabulation table (see Table 1 in the sample quantitative paper at the end of this chapter), and a correlation matrix (not shown). In each type of table, one variable is designated as the row variable and the other as the column variable.

Although most instructors will expect students to use a statistical software program to calculate the means or cross-tabulation tables, Figure 8–2 presents a very simple table based on a calculation of means or averages to show the relationship between two variables to serve as an example. In Figure 8–2 we use date characteristic as the row variable and gender as the column vari-

FIGURE 8–2

SAMPLE TABLE OF MEANS

Table 1. Mean Level of Importance of Five Date Characteristics by Gender

Date Characteristics	Males (N = 15)	Females (N = 15)
Physical Attractiveness	4.6	3.1
Personality	3.0	3.9
Sense of Humor	2.5	3.2
Potential Occupational Success	1.4	4.5
Attitude Similarity	2.2	2.4

able. We designate in parentheses the number of male and female respondents. In preparing this table, we sorted the questionnaires into two piles: one for males and one for females. Then, *separately for each pile*, we added together the numerical scores given by every respondent for each date characteristic. We divided each sum by the number of students in the pile. For example, the responses of the 15 males in pile 1 for the date characteristic "physical attractiveness" summed to 69 ($5 + 4 + 4 + 5 + 4 + 5 + 4 + 5 + 5 + 5 + 4 + 5 + 5 + 4 + 5 = 69$). We divided 69 by the number of the respondents in the pile to obtain the average score for males ($69 \div 15 = 4.6$). We repeated this procedure for each date characteristic. We then did all the same calculations for females. The table reports the mean level of importance of each date characteristic for males and females separately. The results show that males place a greater importance on physical attractiveness (mean = 4.6) than do females (mean = 3.1), while females place greater importance on potential occupational success (mean = 4.5) than do males (mean = 1.4).

Try creating a mock table for analyzing and presenting your results. That is, try to specify which variable you will use as your row variable and which variable will be your column variable, then decide whether you want the numbers in the cells to be percentages or averages. Making a mock table before you use software to run your statistical analyses will help you to better understand the results you will get and whether they support your hypotheses. Software makes it is easy for students to generate lots of output but does not make it easy to understand what the tables and statistics mean. Making a mock table ahead of time will help you to know what to look for and how to interpret the results you generate. But first it will be necessary to determine the type or level of measurement of your variables: are they nominal, ordinal, interval, or ratio? This will allow you to decide which statistical tests can be appropriately calculated.

WRITING THE OTHER SECTIONS OF YOUR PAPER: Methods, Results, and Discussion

THE METHODS SECTION

The methods section immediately follows the literature review and should contain three subparts: sample, measures, and procedure. Each subpart should be labeled with an italicized heading at the left margin. Begin the methods section by describing your sample.

Describing Your Sample

It is important to specify the population you studied. Many people, including beginning sociology students, don't understand how results can be different in different samples. Sometimes sampling bias can be obvious: for example, a sample of sociology students will report significantly different career aspirations than a sample of engineering students. But usually, the bias is more subtle. Thus experienced sociologists will typically respond to reports of quantitative studies with "What is the sample?"

In describing your sample discuss in detail how it was selected from the population. Did you randomly select respondents—that is, give every member of the population an equal chance of being included in the sample—or did you select whomever you could get? If respondents were randomly selected, describe the steps you took to ensure randomness (for example, tossing a coin or systematically selecting every fifth respondent). If you are a more advanced student, did you stratify your sample on any particular variable? If you obtained your data from secondary or archival sources, describe how those data were collected originally.

Describe all the relevant characteristics of your sample including age, gender, and race. If you had to eliminate any subjects because of incomplete data or other reasons, state the number and the reason. Specify the final overall sample size and the size of each group.

Describing Your Measures

If you obtained your data from secondary or archival sources, describe how the variables were measured. If you performed a structured observation, describe the behaviors, types of people, situations, and so forth that you observed.

If you used a questionnaire or an interview, state whether you used closed-ended or open-ended questions, questions developed by you, or questions adapted from previous research. If you used existing scales or indexes, include information about their validity and reliability, if available. Validity refers to the extent to which the questions actually measure what they are supposed to measure. Reliability refers to the stability of measurements taken at different times.

In the body of the paper, quote the actual question(s) used to operationally define each variable. If several questions were used, as in the construction of an index or a scale, give a sample of the questions and include the others in a table or an appendix. For example: "Gender-role attitudes were measured by agreement–disagreement with 20 statements, such as 'The woman's place is in the home' and 'I would vote for a woman presidential candidate' (see Appendix A)." If the questions were closed-ended, state the range of the response scale and describe the points on the scale. For example, you might state that you used "a five-point Likert Scale ranging from 1) not at all to 5) extremely." If you averaged the responses to several questions to form an index, state what the high and low scores on the index signify. For example: "A high score on the gender-role index indicates liberal gender role attitudes; a low score indicates conservative attitudes." If the questions were open-ended, describe the coding scheme that you used.

Describing Your Procedure

If you are conducting a secondary analysis of existing data, describe the procedure used by the researchers who collected the data; if you collected your own data, identify the method you used. Describe when (time of day,

day of week, date, where (the geographic location, type of institution, building), and under what circumstances the study took place. This information is especially important if the study was conducted in a field setting.

If you conducted an experiment, be sure to also specify the design. Discuss the procedure by which the independent variable(s) was (were) manipulated and the instructions given to respondents in each group. Specify any additional precautions taken to control extraneous variables or to exclude bias from your sample. For example, did you randomly assign respondents to experimental conditions? If you employed confederates (accomplices), describe who they were, what they did, and whether they were kept "blind to" (ignorant of) the hypotheses.

Whichever method you chose, summarize each step of your data collection. A good rule of thumb is to describe your methods in enough detail that another researcher could replicate your study.

THE RESULTS SECTION

Discuss how you examined the relationship between your variables. Did you count the number of people who gave each type of response, or did you average the scores of several people? If you calculated percentages or averages, state the number of people used as the denominator in your calculations.

If you have a large amount of data to report, consider displaying it in a table or figure. Put each table or figure on a separate page at the end of the paper following the list of references. Each table should be numbered consecutively. The word "Table" and the number should be bold and end with a period and be followed by a descriptive title that will explain the content of the table without the reader having to refer to the text. The table number and title line should be flush with the left margin (see Figure 8–3). For figures, the number and descriptive title should also be flush with the left margin and bold, but they should be positioned below the graph or diagram (see Figure 8–4). Figures should also be numbered consecutively. In the body of the paper, refer to each table or figure by number; then explain it. Remember that the numbers presented in the table never speak for themselves.

FIGURE 8–3

SAMPLE TABLE OF PERCENTAGES

Table 1. Gender Role Attitudes by Gender of Respondent

Gender Role Attitudes	Gender of Respondent	
	Male (N = 100)	Female (N = 100)
Liberal	55%	85%
Traditional	45	15
TOTAL	100%	100%

FIGURE 8–4

SAMPLE FIGURE

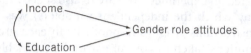

Figure 1. Measurement Model of Gender Role Attitudes

Another way to present your results is by using graphs or charts. Often visual aids can dramatically illustrate relationships between variables. You can use one of the many computer graphics programs that are available. The best known of these programs for the advanced student are IBM SPSS, STATA, and SAS. Programs such as Microsoft's Excel can be most useful for the less-advanced student. Whether you should use a bar chart, a line graph, or a causal model will depend on the type of data that you have and the analyses you perform. Ask your instructor for suggestions on the best way to present your results.

If your assignment required statistical analyses, state the statistical tests performed, their critical values, degrees of freedom, significance levels, and the direction of the results. For example: "The relationship between gender-role attitudes and gender of respondent is reported in Table 1. The results of a chi-square test indicate that a significantly greater proportion of females (85%) than males (55%) hold liberal gender-role attitudes (x^2 = 24.24, d.f. = 100, $p < .01$)." In your discussion section, you will explain the results of the statistical analysis in more detail.

THE DISCUSSION SECTION

The discussion section is where you will tie your results back into your research questions or hypotheses. What were the answers to your research questions? Did the data support any of your hypotheses? Remember that the statistical significance of your findings does not indicate the theoretical, substantive, or practical significance of your findings. The latter is a judgment you must make in the discussion section. What does a relationship between X and Y mean in the larger theoretical context? How do your findings compare with previous research? That is, are your findings consistent or inconsistent with those found by other researchers? What has the study contributed to the existing body of literature on this topic? What are the practical implications of your findings, if any? What ethical issues were raised?

What is the internal and external validity of your study? That is, to what extent does your study provide an adequate test of your hypotheses? Can your findings be generalized to other populations? Discuss any methodological or design flaws, particularly if your hypotheses are not supported. Make suggestions for improving future research. If the study is methodologically sound, how can you account for any unexpected findings? Do the data support an alternative theory?

What conclusions can you draw? What direction should further research on this topic take?

THE TITLE

Now that you've completed the main sections of your paper, you will be able to come up with a good descriptive title. It should be short (rarely more than 12 words) and include the theoretical perspective taken and/or the major variables examined (both independent and dependent, where appropriate). (For guidelines on formatting your title page see Part 4.)

THE ABSTRACT

The abstract, usually about 100 to 200 words in length, is a very brief summary of your paper. It describes the problem, methods, sample, results, and conclusions of your study and should contain only ideas or information already discussed in the body of the paper. The abstract belongs on a separate page following the title page. For a heading, type and left-justify ABSTRACT using all capital letters; triple-space between the heading and the body of the abstract, and indent the first line. Although almost always included in a journal article, an abstract may not be required by your instructor.

THE LIST OF REFERENCES

If no specific journal style is required, follow the reference formatting guidelines provided in Chapter 5. Only include the sources you actually cite in the body of your paper. The list of references should appear on a separate page at the end of your paper (see page 9 of the sample student paper at the end of this chapter for an example).

THE APPENDIX

The appendixes (also called appendices) are optional. Some instructors may want you to include your questionnaire, observation checklist, instructions to respondents, raw data, statistical calculations, or other items in an appendix. Each appendix should be numbered or lettered and given a descriptive title. The appendixes, when included, go after the list of references. See Part 4 for information on how to format an appendix.

SUGGESTED READINGS

Babbie, Earl R. 2013. *The Practice of Social Research.* 13th ed. Belmont, CA: Wadsworth Publishing Co.

Babbie, Earl R., Fred S. Halley, William E. Wagner III, and Jeanne S. Zaino. 2013. *Adventures in Social Research: Data Analysis Using IBM SPSS Statistics.* 8th ed. Thousand Oaks, CA: Sage Publications, Inc.

Chambliss, Daniel F., Russell K. Schutt. 2013. *Making Sense of the Social World: Methods of Investigation.* 4th ed. Thousand Oaks, CA: Sage Publications, Inc

A SAMPLE STUDENT PAPER

The following sample quantitative research paper, a study of gender stereotyping in magazine advertisements, was written by Shannon Prior for an undergraduate course in writing for sociology. Shannon's study reveals that women are portrayed stereotypically in the advertisements of women's magazines, regardless of their race or ethnicity.

Shannon's assignment required her to review the literature on a topic, design a study, and construct measures; however, she only had to simulate rather than collect the data. She included this simulated "raw data" in Appendix B (not shown), allowing the instructor to verify her tabulations.

Because Shannon wrote this paper for a class in writing rather than in research methods, the purpose of the assignment was to demonstrate critical thinking about a sociological topic starting from the formulation of a research question and/or hypothesis to the analysis, interpretation, and discussion of findings. Thus, there was less emphasis on the mechanics of collecting data than on the logic behind the entire research and writing process.

Shannon reviewed the relevant literature on stereotyping in magazine advertisements and developed her main hypotheses to address questions raised by this review. Shannon went beyond other studies by analyzing gender stereotypes of African American and Hispanic women, in addition to white women in magazine advertisements. Thus, this work is located within an ongoing discussion but also contains something original, both of which are important considerations in designing sociological research.

The paper follows a journal article format and is based on simulated quantitative results from an archival study. Notice that it contains the major and minor sections discussed in this chapter: title page, abstract, review of the literature, methods (including subsections on the sample, measures, and procedure), results, and discussion. Shannon also provides a table that presents important results in an easily read format. Her list of references appears toward the end of the paper, but it should have been placed just before her table and appendixes. Our comments detail other important features of the paper as well as ways in which it could be improved.

OUR COMMENTS

Stereotypes of African American, Hispanic, and White Women
in Magazine Advertisements

Shannon Prior
Sociology 301
Dr. Giarrusso
December 18, 2006

Because of the length of her paper, Shannon includes a title page. Shannon correctly begins numbering the pages of her paper after the title page.

Shannon's title appropriately identifies the dependent variable (stereotypes) and the independent variable (race/ethnicity), and hints at the method (examining magazines); however, the title is ambiguous because it does not identify the kinds of stereotypes investigated, whether these stereotypes are racial/ethnic stereotypes, class stereotypes, or gender stereotypes. Because her paper is about gender stereotypes, this topic of gender stereotypes should be specified in the title.

According to the *ASA Style Guide* (2010), Shannon should have centered her name and her university affiliation under the title of her paper.

Shannon includes an abstract of her paper. In less than 200 words she describes the purpose of the paper, the methods, and the results. Because Shannon follows the *ASA Style Guide* (2010), she left-justifies, bolds, and capitalizes all the letters of the heading. However, she incorrectly begins the fourth sentence with a numeral instead of writing it out. Also, she could strengthen her abstract by adding a concluding sentence.

A common error is capitalizing the word "white." According to the *ASA Style Guide*, the words "black" or "white" should not be capitalized; however, it is appropriate to capitalize the words "African American," "Asian," and "Hispanic" because these names represent groups with a common geographic location or language.

ABSTRACT

Research by Lindner (2004) indicates that women have been consistently stereotyped in magazine advertisements since the 1950s. However, her research does not address how women of different races are stereotyped. A content analysis of African American, Hispanic, and White women's magazine advertisements is conducted to compare the stereotypes of each group. 120 advertisements are analyzed using the coding categories relative size, function ranking, licensed withdrawal, body display, location, and objectification. The results show that all groups of women are stereotyped. Advertisements of white women are slightly more likely than advertisements of other women to contain licensed withdrawal and body display. Objectification occurs most frequently in all groups.

1

The power of advertising is clear. The fact that companies annually expend over $200 billion on advertising is a testament to its power and prevalence in our society (Kilbourne 1999). Advertising not only sells products, it also sells images (Baker 2005). Too often these images are stereotypes of women and minorities. These portrayals, whether good or bad, influence our perceptions of the people in our society. For these reasons, the study of minorities and women in advertising is the focus of this research.

Taylor, Lee, and Stern (1995) explore the portrayal of minorities in magazines by conducting a content analysis of four types of magazines (business, women's, general interest, and technical). The researchers analyze the types of roles (major, minor, background, etc.) minorities are cast in and the types of products they are selling. The authors conclude that some stereotypes still persist. African Americans are overrepresented in minor or background roles. Asian Americans are consistently represented as tech-savvy workaholics while Hispanic Americans are either nonexistent or somewhere in the background. Although the study includes women's magazines in their content analysis, they do not provide a specific analysis of gender-role stereotypes.

To gain a better understanding of gender portrayals in advertising, I consulted Katharina Lindner's (2004) longitudinal study of women in *Time* and *Vogue* magazine advertisements. The study utilizes Goffman's frame analysis and coding scheme, which is designed to detect subtle messages in advertising. Lindner finds that 78% of the advertisements portray women stereotypically. The study finds decreases over time in certain categories of stereotypes. For instance, the feminine touch category in which the woman depicted is touching her hair, face, or clothing in an unnatural manner or stroking an object declines throughout the years. However, Lindner was surprised to find that the other types of stereotypes measured remain relatively stable over time. Overall, objectification, when the woman's sole

Shannon begins the literature review section by providing a statement of the problem: advertisers often use stereotypes to sell products. However, at this point it is still unclear whether Shannon will be focusing on gender stereotypes or racial/ethnic stereotypes.

Aptly, Shannon provides a description of a journal article; however, this description would be stronger if she revealed the gender of the individuals studied in the advertisements. Also, she should have stated whether her own study was going to examine one or both genders.

Shannon's critique of the study—that the findings cannot be generalized to minority women—shows critical-thinking skills. Additionally, she is careful to give the operational definitions of the gender-role stereotypes that are studied, that is, she specifies how the variables are measured.

Shannon provides another description of an empirical journal article, clarifying how the dependent variable in this article differs from the ones in the other articles she reviewed. It appears that the Baker article is not as relevant to her topic as the previous article by Lindner, but there may not have been another article closely related to her topic.

purpose is to be looked at, occurs most frequently. Although this study provides insight into gender portrayals, it only includes publications directed toward a mainstream, predominantly White audience. Therefore, the results do not apply to minority women.

In contrast to Lindner's study, Christina N. Baker (2005) studies the portrayal of African American and White women's sexuality in advertising. She conducted a content analysis of African American- and White-oriented men's and women's magazines to compare the portrayals of African American and White women's sexuality. Included in her study is an analysis of the role of women and the authority of the women in relation to the men. In women's magazines, Baker finds that African American women are more likely to be portrayed as independent compared to White women. White women are more likely to be portrayed as "partners" or have their faces hidden, signifying subordination. However, the results are not generalizable because Baker only includes advertisements that display women in a sexual manner.

It is clear from the previous research that White and minority women are stereotyped in magazine advertisements. These stereotypes are not simply images, they are powerful messages that "depict for us not necessarily how we actually behave as men and women but how we think men and women behave" (Gornick 1979:7). Therefore, I wish to further explore the types and frequencies of gender stereotypes in magazine advertisements. I contribute to the literature by examining and comparing the stereotypes of African American, Hispanic, and White women in African American-, Hispanic-, and White- oriented women's magazines.

Based on the literature reviewed, I hypothesize that all groups of women will be stereotyped. Based specifically on Lindner's (2004) study, I hypothesize that objectification will occur most frequently out of all the

Appropriately, Shannon offers two hypotheses, each regarding the expected frequency of various gender stereotypes; she is able to provide "educated guesses" about the likelihood of these findings because there is adequate literature available about her topic. Conversely, because there is not enough literature on "which race/ethnic group will be stereotyped most frequently" and "in what ways" for her to render hypotheses, she poses these as research questions.

stereotype categories. Due to the lack of research on the topic, I explore rather than hypothesize which racial group will be stereotyped most frequently and in what ways.

METHODS

Sample

A content analysis is conducted to examine and compare the portrayals of African American, Hispanic, and White women in magazine advertisements. Since minority women are underrepresented in mainstream magazine advertising, I analyze African American- and Hispanic-oriented magazines in addition to a mainstream or White-oriented magazines. I do so in the hope of obtaining a close to equal amount of Black, Hispanic, and White women. I chose *Redbook* for White women, *Latina* for Hispanic women, and *Essence* for Black women. All of the magazines contain similar topic matter including sections on beauty, fashion, sex, and health. The sample of advertisements is taken from the January and June issues published in 2005. I chose a winter and summer month to control for any bias that one season might create. For example, summer months would most likely contain more advertisements with body display.

Measures

Goffman's (1997) coding scheme categories relative size, function ranking, and licensed withdrawal are used to analyze the advertisements. In addition, Umiker-Sebeok's (1996) category location, Lindner's (2004) category objectification, and Kang's (1997) category body display are used. See Appendix A for the full list of the categories including their operational definitions.

Although for most research studies, the sample refers to people, in an archival study, the sample refers to existing documents. Importantly, Shannon specifies how she selected her sample (magazines): she chose magazines that would provide her with a close-to-equal repre-sentation of women from each race/ethnic group. Moreover, she shows her critical-thinking skills by selecting the January and June issues to control for possible seasonal biases in the advertisements.

Shannon effectively integrates the coding schemes of different researchers in examin-ing her hypotheses and answering her research questions. She also provides an operational definition of each type of stereo-type to be investigated in an appendix at the end of her paper.

Shannon provides further specification about how the advertisements are selected and coded. To her credit, she trained two coders to examine the data and made sure that there was high inter-rater reliability before having the coders analyze the rest of the advertisements.

Shannon uses the word "significant," however, she does not mean the term "statistically significant," which means that the differences found could not be attributable to chance. To avoid any possible ambiguity here, Shannon should have substituted the word "noteworthy" or "noticeable" when she was revising her final draft.

The fourth sentence of the paragraph begins incorrectly with a numeral. Shannon could have eliminated this error by putting a semicolon at the end of the previous sentence and joining them to make one sentence or by writing out the number in words: "Thirteen percent."

Procedure

Only full-page advertisements containing at least one woman with or without one or more men were coded. At least one woman in the advertisement had to appear to be Black, Hispanic, or White. Other minority women were excluded from this study due to the lack of a comparable magazine that targets them. Two coders were trained to use the coding scheme and were not informed of the exact purpose of the study. 25% of the sample was analyzed by each coder. The results were compared and inconsistencies were resolved. Each coder then analyzed half of the sample.

RESULTS

Table 1 displays the percentage of each gender stereotype by race/ethnicity. I found that African American, Hispanic, and White women are all consistently stereotyped. There were significant differences in the frequencies of stereotypes based on race with the exception of the categories location and objectification. I also found particular categories of stereotypes to be more prevalent than others among all women tested.

To obtain percentages of the stereotypes for each group of women, I took the total number of times the stereotype occurred within that race and divided it by the total number of women in that group. To calculate the average percentage of stereotype categories, I added the percentages of each category and divided it by three. See Appendix B for the raw data.

I averaged the percentages for the three race groups to determine which categories occurred most frequently overall. The categories relative size and function ranking occurred the least among all of the categories at 6.7%. Location occurred in 10% of the advertisements. 13.3% of the

5

advertisements contained the stereotype licensed withdrawal. Body display occurred in 23.3% of the sample. Objectification was the most frequent stereotype, occurring in 40% of the advertisements.

There were significant differences among the women in the categories relative size, function ranking, licensed withdrawal, and body display.

0% of the advertisements of White women contained relative size or function ranking. In contrast, 10% of advertisements depicting African American women and 10% depicting Hispanic women contained relative size and function ranking. Advertisements depicting White women contained more instances of licensed withdrawal (20%) and body display (30%) compared to African American (10% and 20%, respectively) and Hispanic (10% and 20%, respectively) women.

DISCUSSION

Whether we acknowledge it or not, advertising permeates almost every aspect of our lives. The images in advertisements define and solidify gender roles (Baker 2005). For these reasons I studied the stereotypes of African American, Hispanic, and White women in magazine advertisements. I hypothesized that each group of women would be stereotyped. This hypothesis was supported by my findings. African American, Hispanic, and White women were stereotyped in almost every category tested. This was consistent with Lindner's (2004) study, which found that 78% of the advertisements examined in *Time* and *Vogue* contained stereotypes of women. This finding was also supported by Baker's (2005) study, which found that African American and White women were stereotyped in White and African American men's and women's magazine advertisements. Although Taylor et al. (1995) found minorities to be stereotyped in magazine advertisements they did not specifically examine stereotypes of

Shannon begins the discussion section by reiterating the reason for her study and reminding the reader of her hypotheses. She then concludes that the data supported her first hypothesis. Moreover, she ties her first finding back to the literature she reviewed at the beginning of her paper by indicating whether her results were consistent with those of other researchers. She is careful to state that the study by Taylor et al. was not similar enough to make a meaningful comparison.

6

women. Therefore, our findings could not be confirmed or denied by their study.

My second hypothesis, that objectification would be the most prevalent stereotype, was supported by my data. Objectification occurred in 40% of the advertisements analyzed, more than any other category. This finding was consistent with Lindner's (2004) study, which also found objectification to be the most common stereotype in *Time* and *Vogue* magazine advertisements. Since Baker (2005) and Taylor et al. (1995) did not use objectification in their content analysis, their studies could not substantiate or deny my second hypothesis.

The prevalence of objectification can be interpreted as a reaction against the economic and social freedoms enjoyed by the modern woman. In Naomi Wolf's (1991) book, *The Beauty Myth,* she argues that the beauty myth, the unattainable image of women perpetuated by the mass media, is a tool of patriarchy. As women have become stronger materially they have been weakened psychologically by the beauty myth (Wolf 1991). This unrealistic ideal of beauty keeps women mentally and physically preoccupied with their bodies (Wolf 1991). This theory was supported by the frequent occurrence of objectification in advertisements. Objectification, which occurs when a woman is depicted for the sole purpose of being looked at, fully acquaints women with the ideal they must strive to attain.

Wolf's theory was also supported by the low occurrence of function ranking and relative size. Function ranking occurs when the man in the advertisement plays a dominant role as a boss or instructor. Relative size occurs when the man in the advertisement is larger or takes up more space than the woman. Both of these stereotypes display more traditional gender roles in which the woman is subordinate to the man. Since the women's movement, these gender roles are considered to be outdated and

> These two paragraphs are very strong because they provide an interpretation of the results. The purpose of the discussion section is to give meaning to the numbers that were presented in the results section, rather than repeating the findings that were reported. Shannon explains how her findings support the idea of a beauty myth.

7

unacceptable to today's woman. Hence, the emergence of the modern beauty myth and the prevalence of more subtle forms of stereotypes like objectification. However, the requirement of a man and woman to be depicted together could also account for the low occurrence of function ranking and relative size.

The high occurrence of objectification can also be explained by economics. Kalle Lasn, the founder of *Adbusters* magazine, argues that advertising starts a vicious cycle. It bolsters our insecurities by bombarding us with unattainable images of beauty and then it "offers us a variety of ways to buy our way back to security" (Lasn 1999:17). For Lasn, the beauty myth does not discriminate based on gender. He argues that because it is more profitable advertisers launch their psychological assault on both men and women.

Although my study was not perfect, the results suggest that women should be aware of the images they are absorbing. Women can resist the psychological assault of the beauty myth by being conscious of the subtle messages conveyed in advertisements. We must also teach our children to be media literate and aware of damaging stereotypes perpetrated by the media. In addition, we can take action by writing letters to advertisers and magazine editors expressing our disapproval of the stereotypes conveyed in their advertisements and magazines.

For the future, it would be interesting to focus on the racial stereotypes present in women's magazines. It would also be interesting to study the stereotypes of men in men's magazines. If stereotypes like objectification are also high, it would mean the beauty myth is less about gender and more about money. I would also like to study stereotypes in teen magazines. It would also be interesting to expose teens to popular advertisements and then test their perceptions of themselves and the opposite sex.

| This is another strong paragraph because Shannon postulates yet another possible explanation of her findings. The two explanations are mutually exclusive, meaning only one of them can be correct. Also, telling the reader about Lasn's credentials as founder of Adbusters effectively supports the credibility of the borrowed explanation cited here. |

| Importantly, Shannon explains the implications of her findings and gives concrete ways to counter the pernicious effect of gender stereotyping in advertising. |

| Shannon proposes several interesting ways to extend her work in future research. Any one of these ideas would be an interesting quantitative research paper topic. |

According to the *ASA Style Guide,* Shannon puts the table on a separate page at the end of her paper; however, she should have put it after the References. By giving the table a descriptive title, the reader can understand what's in the table without having to read the text. Shannon includes the sample size of each race/ethnic group and gives the total percent for each column; this indicates that race/ethnicity is the independent variable and that the type of gender stereotype is the dependent variable.

Table 1. Type of Gender Stereotype by Race/Ethnicity of Women in Magazine Advertisements

Type of Gender Stereotype	Race/Ethnicity			
	African American (N = 10)	Hispanic (N =10)	White (N =10)	Average of Three Groups
Relative Size	10%	10%	0%	6.7%
Function Rank	10%	10%	0%	6.7%
Licensed Withdrawal	10%	10%	20%	13.3%
Body Display	20%	20%	30%	23.3%
Location	10%	10%	10%	10%
Objectification	40%	40%	40%	40%
Total	100%	100%	100%	

APPENDIX A

Operational Definitions of Coding Categories

1. Relative Size. In advertisements with both men and women present, the man is larger than the woman and more space in the ad is used by him.

2. Function Ranking. When both men and women are depicted, the man plays a dominant part as a superior or instructor.

3. Licensed Withdrawal. The woman is mentally not present. Her gaze is off in the distance or she is smiling or laughing, covering her face or mouth.

4. Body Display. The woman depicted is wearing revealing clothing or no clothing at all.

5. Location. The woman is depicted in a domestic or unidentifiable environment. Examples would be a kitchen, bedroom, bathroom, or a setting that does not lend itself to any purposeful activities.

6. Objectification. Occurs when being looked at is the major purpose of the woman depicted.

> According to the *ASA Style Guide,* Shannon should have put the appendix on a separate page after the References. However, she does provide the appendix with a descriptive title.

Shannon uses the term "references" rather than "bibliography" because she includes only those articles and books that she actually cites (see Chapter 5). A bibliography is rarely appropriate for a quantitative journal article, unless indicated by your instructor. Shannon follows the *ASA Style Guide* in formatting the bibliographic information for the articles and books she cites.

REFERENCES

Baker, Christina N. 2005. "Images of Women's Sexuality in Advertisements: A Content Analysis of Black- and White-Oriented Women's and Men's Magazines." *Sex Roles* 52(1–2):13–27.

Goffman, E. 1979. *Gender Advertisements*. Cambridge, MA: Harvard University Press.

Gornick, V. 1979. "Introduction." Pp. vii–ix in *Gender Advertisements* by E. Goffman. Cambridge, MA: Harvard University Press.

Kang, M.E. 1997. "The Portrayal of Women's Images in Magazine Advertisements: Goffman's Gender Analysis Revisited." *Sex Roles* 37(11–12):979–97.

Kilbourne, Jean. 1999. *Can't Buy My Love: How Advertising Changes the Way We Think and Feel*. New York: Touchstone.

Lasn, Kalle. 1999. *Culture Jam: How to Reverse America's Suicidal Consumer Binge—And Why We Must*. New York: Harper Collins Publishers.

Lindner, Katharina. 2004. "Images of Women in General Interest and Fashion Magazine Advertisements from 1955 to 2002." *Sex Roles* 51(7–8):409–21.

Taylor, Charles R., Yu Yung Lee, and Barbara B. Stern. 1995. "Portrayals of African, Hispanic, and Asian Americans in Magazine Advertising." *American Behavioral Scientist* 38(4):608–21.

Umiker-Sebeok, J. 1996. "Power and Construction of Gendered Spaces." *International Review of Sociology* 6(3):389–404.

Wolf, Naomi. [1991] 2003. "The Beauty Myth." Pp. 515–524 in *Signs of Life in the USA: Readings on Popular Culture for Writers*, edited by Sonia Maasik and Jack Solomon. Boston, MA: Bedford/St.Martin's Press.

Consistent with the *ASA Style Guide*, Shannon includes both the volume number and the issue number of the journal articles in her references.

Following the *ASA Style Guide*, with the exception of New York, Shannon includes both the city and state for all book references.

11

C H A P T E R

N I N E

The Qualitative Research Paper

Qualitative analysis transforms data into findings. No formula exists for that transformation. Guidance, yes. But no recipe. Direction can and will be offered, but the final destination remains unique for each inquirer, known only when—and if—arrived at.

—MICHAEL QUINN PATTON

Sociologists don't always agree with one another about what makes a research method "qualitative." Some researchers suggest that qualitative methods are defined by what they are not: they do not involve counting or measuring the social phenomenon of interest as do the quantitative methods discussed in the previous chapter. Qualitative research is sometimes thought of as a step in the scientific process that's used when too little is known about a research topic to even develop a general hypothesis. So, to begin, a quantitative researcher can identify variables to observe and then use direct observation and in-depth interviews to deduce a hypothesis. The observations that support that hypothesis and how it is all related to broader sociological concepts can be written up in a format similar to quantitative studies.

Others argue that qualitative methods take a distinctive approach to exploring the social world by setting out to represent the process of social life from the point of view of the participants or members in the setting or field being investigated. Those advocating a fundamental difference between qualitative and quantitative methods use qualitative methods to understand *how* things happen rather than *why* they happen; they tend to emphasize the experience of the participants more than the perspective of the observer. Studies about *how* things happen often produce new theoretical insights, but are most noted for their vivid descriptions of social scenes and transactions. In other words, even after collecting data, the researcher rarely attempts to propose a hypothesis about why something happens in the social world; instead the researcher attempts to uncover what happens in a social setting, *how* social relationships are conducted, and what those events and relationships mean to those involved.

WHAT IS HIGH QUALITY IN A QUALITATIVE PAPER?

As you learned in the previous chapter, quantitative methods in social science have a highly developed set of conventions about how research is conducted

and how to identify high-quality research. But with qualitative methods, the standards for excellence are not as widely agreed upon and readers are more likely to disagree about what books or papers are excellent. Nonetheless, we want to highlight some criteria that we think are important for creating a high-quality qualitative paper and that are relatively uncontroversial.

+ The qualitative paper emphasizes a sociological theme or themes. Too often writers of qualitative papers want to include everything they have learned or observed in their paper whether or not it is related to the theme of their research. An author needs to be able to say in one or two sentences what the sociological theme of her or his research is, and show how everything in the paper directly or indirectly contributes to it. Often, it seems so obvious to the author what the theme is and how everything in the paper relates that it is left up to the reader to make sociological sense of data.

+ It makes sense of data with sociological concepts. This is related to the first point. Most description begins with ordinary (nonsociological) language. It is not that ordinary language lacks theory, but that the implicit theory is folk sociology—the commonsense notions that people have about how people relate to one another. A sociologist translates commonsense categories into sociological concepts. For example, an everyday description might be "a student is talking with a professor about her grade." But a sociologist might see two people in different roles negotiating the exercise of authority and legitimacy. The sociologist can apply insights learned from other cases when people in different roles negotiate the exercise of authority such as doctor–patient relations, employer–employee relations, or parent–child relations. And he or she might then suggest how the observations of the student and professor offer insights about those other interactions. Doing this intellectual work back and forth between observations and generalizations is at the heart of sociological thinking.

+ It connects to what other scholars have learned. Remember that all research, whether by a beginning student or a professional scholar, is cumulative, building on what others have previously discovered. For the example of the student and professor discussing a grade, a sociologist would want to connect findings to what others have said about student–professor relations as well as other authority relations.

+ It includes thick description. Thick description is a term that social scientists use for detailed description of people or settings that communicate the feel of what is observed to capture a sense of the whole. So excellent qualitative researchers must develop some of the sensitivity of novelists. The trick is to separate relevant details from extraneous details. Does it matter what sort of clothes people are wearing, what expressions they make, or what the art is on the wall where they are? There are no quick answers. But the author should know what difference included details do make. Part of the answer will be what difference it makes to the people who inhabit the setting being observed.

Thick description usually is sensitive to the meaning of interactions and events to the people being studied. Usually writing up description works best when the author frequently intersperses interpretation and sociological sense-making with straight description, not offering all the description and then creating the sociological sense.

TYPES OF QUALITATIVE PAPERS

Qualitative methods involve some sort of overt or explicit data such as observations, interviews, or archival research. General research papers and textual analysis papers have been discussed in earlier chapters. Many of the lessons from those chapters are relevant here as well as some of the specifics, especially the pointers about how to format papers. The three-point essay discussed in Chapter 7 can be used for most qualitative papers. Here are some of the main types of qualitative papers, though these types have some overlap among them.

+ **Case study.** As the name implies, case studies involve a single case— a person, couple, organization, incident, neighborhood, or society. Sometimes a case study can be an exercise to show that a student understands sociological concepts, for example, using their parents as a case of marriage (and perhaps divorce). But it is more ambitious to use cases to identify anomalies in existing theory or elaborate theory. A negative case study finds a case that doesn't fit sociological expectations and suggests how the theory would have to be altered. For example, a case study of an underfunded school in a poor neighborhood that sent most of its students to college would require us to rethink the relationship between social class and the quality of education. While some negative case studies might directly challenge existing theory, more often they will help refine our theories. A sociologist might find that what was unusual about the school just mentioned is that the parents, even though relatively poor, were very active in the school, forcing our theories about social class and education to include parental involvement as a relevant factor. Case studies can be written up in a three-point essay, a narrative account, or a journal format.
+ **Comparative analysis.** Here two or more cases are studied in depth as in a case study, but they are selected to be similar or different on important variables. For example, a sociologist might be interested to learn why Canada and the United States, which are similar in so many ways, have very different kinds of medical systems. Canada is a state-run health system and the United States depends mostly on a private health system. Comparative analysis is typically used for organizations, large aggregates of people like races, and entire societies; in other words, macrolevel units. They are typically written up in journal format.
+ **Interview study.** Case studies and other kinds of qualitative papers often involve interviews, which are structured conversations with people be-

ing studied. Rather than strict questionnaires or surveys, interviews are more conversational, with the researcher asking all research subjects a set of broad questions in a fluid format. Interviews are typically transcribed word for word and then studied in detail to find recurrent themes. There is no particular paper format for interview studies, though the journal format is the most common format.

+ **Archival study.** Analogous to the interview, an archival study can "interview" documents, newspapers, diaries, letters, organizational files, or reports, in the sense that the sociologist hopes to learn about social life from a bunch of information, much of which will be discarded. Even images, sound recordings, objects, and artifacts can reveal important insights about social life. The difference, of course, is that we can't ask questions to the archive. The information is either there or it is not. But the advantage is that archival sources often leave traces of social life that participants themselves may not be aware of. For example, letters between husbands and wives may reveal assumptions about gender that the men and women involved would never have articulated directly. Archival studies can be quantitative, but are more often qualitative. How they are written up depends on the research design of the study they are part of.

+ **Ethnography.** Ethnography is a method based on direct observation of the social world in natural settings or in-depth interviews that reflect direct knowledge of natural settings. Ethnographic research is one of several types of qualitative methods used by sociologists, as well as by their colleagues in other fields such as anthropology, education, social work, journalism, and management. We chose to focus on ethnography in this chapter because it is one of the most common styles of qualitative research. In addition, the field research techniques used in ethnographic research are key to other qualitative methods.[1]

[1] For more information on the range and nature of research methods considered "qualitative," see Denzin, Norman K. and Yvonna S. Lincoln. 2005. *The SAGE Handbook of Qualitative Research.* 3rd ed. Thousand Oaks, CA: Sage Publications; or Merriam, Sharan B. 2002. *Qualitative Research in Practice: Examples for Discussion and Analysis.* San Francisco, CA: Jossey-Bass.

GOALS AND METHODS OF ETHNOGRAPHIC FIELD RESEARCH

Ethnographic research seeks to understand both familiar and unfamiliar social settings. In undertaking ethnographic research, a researcher uses his or her sociological imagination to find the connection between the individual, private experience, and wider society. Ethnographic research can allow you to see how society's institutions, such as the police, the judicial system, and the health-care system are enacted by individuals in everyday settings. It can also allow you to see patterns and processes that often pass unnoticed in common social interactions and how they relate to broader sociological concepts.

The ethnographic researcher conducts research by closely observing what people are doing, by talking with them casually, or by participating in activities with them.

In an *ethnographic field research* project, your data come from observing or interacting with people in everyday social settings, known as "the field." The data are gathered when a researcher visits the setting (allowing him or her to conduct *observational* research), takes part in the setting's activities (called *participant observation*), and sometimes *interviews* participants in the setting. If interviews are conducted, the ethnographer uses open-ended questions to encourage respondents to answer with their own words. The method used for ethnographic research depends on the setting, its inhabitants, and on the researcher's personal style.

As ethnographic research seeks to observe and describe social settings and interactions rather than identify cause-and-effect relationships, ethnographers often begin their research with *how* or *what* questions rather than *why* (as described above). Examples of these questions include: What do police officers do while on duty? How do those sharing an elevator ride deal with one another when space is limited? How do students act in academic settings?

Ethnographic observation and analysis are skills developed through practice. Think of the difference between watching basketball or soccer game for for the first time and how a coach watches game films: the novice observer sees only a blur of action while the experienced observer or coach can see subtle but important movements and relationships. In the same way, ethnographers may begin their research projects seeing social interaction in their setting as a blur but develop their understanding of the setting over time.

REVIEWING THE LITERATURE

Some instructors prefer their students go into the field with as few preconceptions as possible and thus do not assign a review of the literature prior to data collection. However, your instructor may prefer you to familiarize yourself with what sociologists already know about your question by conducting an overview of relevant research on your subject. In this case, refer to the guidelines for library research in Chapter 4 (p. 45).

COLLECTING YOUR DATA

UNDERSTAND THE ASSIGNMENT

It's important that you understand the instructions for your assignment. Where are you supposed to go? What are you to look for? Is there a specific question you should address?

The most common mistake students make in conducting an ethnographic research project is that they focus so intently on describing a setting that they neglect to discuss it from a sociological perspective. Be sure you understand whether the assignment requires you to provide a detailed account of the interaction being observed, or if you are to demonstrate your ability to apply course concepts to what you see, or both. As always, ask your instructor for any necessary clarification.

PLAN AHEAD

1. Begin early in the quarter or semester. Field data cannot always be collected predictably or on short notice. Furthermore, you may have to return to your field setting several times to gather additional information or to gain a better understanding of your data.

2. Make arrangements to interview and/or observe. While you may be apprehensive about obtaining permission, you will find that most people are receptive to showing or telling you about their lives. You can assure them that, if they prefer, their identities will remain anonymous. When scheduling your observation or interview, allow plenty of time. Unanticipated events may occur, your subject may begin to talk at length about some particularly interesting topic, or you may think of additional questions. Also, allow time to record, transcribe, or elaborate on notes immediately after the contact.

3. Plan how you will record your data (a summary of recording options follows later in this chapter). The data collection methods you choose will depend on the situation, your personal style, and the ethical constraints of the situation. Whatever approach you take, be prepared with adequate supplies, including laptop, paper, pens, pencils, and a backup recording device.

4. Be sensitive to ethical concerns of doing research. You have an obligation to notify people that they are being studied and to give them an opportunity to remain anonymous. In the past it was common to study people without their knowledge or to misrepresent the purpose of the research to participants. Such practices are now considered unethical. It is best to avoid any research situation in which people could conceivably be put in danger or in which you might witness illegal activity. Finally, be sure to follow the procedures established by your college's Office for the Protection of Research Subjects or Institutional Review Board, which might require you to submit your research plan for approval or to obtain written permission from those you observe or interview. Consult your instructor for details.

LOOK AND LISTEN

Although you may know a lot about the setting and the interactions you observe, you can gain even deeper sociological insight if you leave behind your previous assumptions and your knowledge about them. Adopt the attitude of a newcomer so you can gain a new perspective on events and experiences.

Don't prematurely reach conclusions about your newly collected observations, rather be attentive to detail, and gather as much valuable information as possible.

When observing, don't presume you know which events or interactions matter most. Be aware of everything that is going on around you: notice your surroundings, the people who are present, the duration of events and activities, etc.

During the interview, consider how the person you are interviewing sees you or what he or she thinks about the questions you pose. How might he or she relate to someone of your age, race/ethnicity, gender, and/or educational level? Your sensitivity to social dynamics will help establish a rapport during the interview, thus putting the interviewee at ease. Guidelines for the interviewing process include:

> *"Mediocrity can talk, but it is for genius to observe."*
>
> Benjamin Disraeli

1. Don't talk excessively. Listen carefully to the respondent's comments.
2. Ask open-ended questions and avoid leading questions that define the respondent's answer.
3. Rather than asking why something happened, concentrate on asking what transpired and how it occurred. "Why" questions often put people on the defensive, making them feel forced to justify their actions or lifestyle. Also, respondents' answers to "how" questions are usually more specific about real events, providing you with concrete examples to describe the setting in detail.
4. Don't overwhelm your interviewee with too many questions. If you are a new interviewer, you may be uncomfortable with silence, but don't rush in with comments, requests for clarification, or further questions if the respondent pauses. Allow the respondent time to think and to complete his or her answer.
5. Encourage the respondent to be specific about the details of events or experiences: Exactly who was involved? What happened? When did it take place? Remember, however, that probing should be gentle and not an interrogation. For example, "Could you tell me more about that?"
6. If you are interviewing a public figure who is used to being interviewed, use some of the tips above to get them beyond their canned answers. They may be used to giving 20- or 30-second sound bites to reporters. Try to be as conversational as you can to get them out of their interview mode.
7. Relax, allow your natural curiosity about your subject to direct you, and *listen*.

RECORD YOUR DATA

Since the final paper you produce will be only as good as your recorded data, it is crucial that you record observations and interview responses accurately, in detail, as soon as possible after the event; otherwise, you can forget or distort what was said or done. Your field notes are an important component of the writing process—especially in ethnography.

In observational research, take notes on what you see or hear as it happens or consider using a camera or cell phone to document your observations. If that is impractical or bothers those you are observing, then write notes on what you observed as soon as possible afterward. You may even want to take periodic note-taking breaks away from the setting during your observation to jot down a few words or phrases that will trigger your memory later. If you are interviewing, it is best to electronically record the conversation and transcribe it. Your obligation as a researcher, however, is to respect the privacy of all subjects by getting written agreement from everyone being recorded. Check with your instructor on any questions regarding these ethical issues.

People are often agreeable and respect your interest in accurately representing the conversation. If subjects seem reluctant to let you record, don't force the issue. Just listen carefully and reconstruct the interview in writing as soon as possible. Don't editorialize in your reporting. Likewise, don't edit your interview to make responses seem more sensible or because something seems "inconsequential." If you edit or editorialize, you may inadvertently omit something significant. Report all the respondents' comments, keeping them in their original order. Be sure to include all your questions and answers.

Make your notes specific; give detailed descriptions of what you observed, did, and/or heard; and give the specifics of who, what, when, and where. How did you feel about the people involved? Remember in ethnographic field research, you are the research instrument; your personal reactions are especially important. It is through your thoughts and feelings and your interactions that you learn about the people and settings you are studying.

You may be required to submit your field notes as an appendix to your paper (see page 167 of Part 4) to provide insight into your observational research or interview. Whether you are submitting your notes or not, keep them legible and organized, and date each entry. The quality of your paper relies on the quality of your field notes and interview notes or transcript.

EXAMPLE OF OBSERVATIONAL FIELD NOTES

The following sample of observational field notes were excerpted from the notes written by Gloria Fong, an undergraduate student in a class on the sociology of student and campus culture at a large university in preparation for her paper, which will be presented later in this chapter. Participants were asked to investigate aspects of student life; Gloria's observations focused on the nonacademic activities of students during lecture and seminar classes.

OUR COMMENTS

EXCERPTS FROM GLORIA'S FIELD NOTES

SEMINAR FIELD NOTES, May 11, 1–3 P.M.

I entered the seminar room through the one and only door. I was nervous about observing, even though I usually attend this class anyway. In the middle of the small room is a large rectangular table with sixteen chairs around it, seven on each long side of the table and two individual chairs at each end of the table. The room is cramped, to say the least. There are fifteen students and one professor. The students sit around the table, and the professor sits at the head of the table, the seat facing opposite the door. A wall of windows is behind the professor, and the other three walls are blackboards.

Two females are each sitting seven seats away from the professor, directly across the table from each other, one on the left and one on the right side of the table. The female on the right side of the table (female A) is a Hispanic female, wearing a white T-shirt and black pants. She has black hair pulled back with black elastic into a ponytail. The female on the left side of the table (female B) is a Caucasian female, wearing a tan sweatshirt and blue jeans. She has long, dark brown hair, and it hangs loosely around her face.

During the seminar meeting, these two females pass back and forth female A's copy of a newspaper clipping and female B's open notebook. I can see that the two students are doing the campus newspaper's daily crossword puzzle together, even though they are across the table from each other. They signal to each other when they need help, and take turns filling in the blanks of the crossword puzzle. They both look up at the professor periodically to see where he is in the room so they do not get caught. Neither of them seems to notice that they are being very obvious with their passing the crossword puzzle and notebooks back and forth across the table. When I asked them about it later, female A said, "We're not trying to

1

> Gloria is careful to identify where and when her observations took place.

> It's normal to be nervous about beginning observations, even in a familiar environment.

> Gloria describes the setting. Throughout her field notes she includes descriptions of all students in the seminar room. The setup turns out to be significant: by noting the seating arrangement, she realizes that students sitting at a distance from the instructor are more likely to engage in nonacademic activities.

> Remember your notes are not a formal treatise. Describe gestures, sounds, and smells to bring the setting or interactions alive.

> Be careful not to make assumptions. It's obvious the two students look up at the instructor, but we don't know why.

Wherever possible make a note of direct quotations right away. Otherwise, paraphrase as accurately as possible.

disrespect the professor, but we just get bored and it's a challenge to try to finish the puzzle. We help each other out."

LECTURE FIELD NOTES, 5/13, 2–3:30 P.M.

As with the seminar setting, Gloria carefully describes the academic setting where her observations occurred. We get a sense of the large room and the distance between students and between students and instructor.

I walked into the large lecture hall through the left set of doors. There are three main sections of seats, a left, right, and middle section. The right and left sections each consist of fourteen rows of seats with three seats across each row. The middle section consists of thirteen rows of seats with eight seats across each row. There are no windows in the room, and the ceilings are much higher than in the seminar room. The professor stands at the front corner of the lecture hall, behind a lectern. Behind the professor is a large movie screen with a picture of lecture notes projected upon it. The class is not full at all, and only the first five rows and the last two rows of the room have students in the seats.

It is important to separate what is obvious, such as the exact words, movements, or gestures that anyone in the same setting would be able to see or hear, and what is assumed, which is what we conclude based on those observations. Gloria is careful to document the actions she observed that led her to conclude the student was intermittently sleeping while taking notes.

One student I observed was an Asian male in a black T-shirt and black pants, wearing a red baseball cap backward, sitting alone in the last row of the lecture hall. The student is hunched over his desk, with his elbows on the desk, his arms supporting his head, and his eyes are closed. His notebook is open on the desk, supporting his arms and head, and he has a black pen uncapped in his right hand. He opens his eyes wide and shakes his head from side to side. He looks to the front of the room when his eyes are open and then looks down at his notebook and begins to write. He writes in his notebook for ten minutes and then rests his head on his arms and closes his eyes again. Five minutes pass and his whole body hunches over the desk. He drops his pen on the floor and does not pick it up. His body moves up and down in rhythm with his breathing. My assumption is that this male student is attempting to take notes, but falls asleep in lecture instead. He is trying to pay attention, but just keeps falling asleep in between his frantic note-taking sessions.

EXAMPLE OF INTERVIEW NOTES

Following is an excerpt from the interview notes that Gloria Fong (GF) jotted down during or immediately after speaking with one of the students (S1) she had observed while researching her paper about college student and campus culture (see pp. 157–164). Although she could have asked for permission to record the interview, Gloria opted to take interview notes instead.

GF: What do you think of attending class?

S1: It's okay—Sometimes kind of boring.

GF: How do you deal with it?

S1: I try really hard to take notes but then I just space out. But I don't want to skip lecture because then I might miss something that is on the final. I stop by and get a newspaper every time I come to this class. I rip out the crossword and put it in my notebook before I walk in. I just can't take notes the whole time so I need something else to do to pass the time.

Gloria's inquiries are phrased as *what* and *how* questions, which elicit better information from interview subjects than *why* questions. If she had asked, "Why don't you pay attention in class?" the student might have felt defensive about sharing her thoughts about classroom behaviors. Also, her questions are open-ended, so they cannot be answered with a *yes* or *no*. As shown in this interview excerpt Gloria's questions paid off; being able to convey the voices of actual students makes Gloria's paper richer and more graphic.

She might have heard more specific responses if she focused her questions. For example, "What do you think of attending class?" is a broad inquiry that generated a general response. She might have learned more detail if she had asked specifically what the subject thought of a particular aspect of attending a college class, such as "What do you do during class besides listening and taking notes on what the instructor says?"

> *"You may have heard the world is made up of atoms and molecules, but it's really made up of stories. When you sit with an individual that's been here, you can give quantitative data a qualitative overlay."*
>
> William Turner

ORGANIZING YOUR DATA

The observations and answers you collect in your fieldwork are the data on which your paper will be based. In this step of research, use the material you have collected to analyze the setting and/or to answer your research question. You will need to identify, sort, and organize segments of your notes, either electronically or on a hard copy. This is an exciting process; as you work with your notes you will notice that the setting you have analyzed reveals information about the nature of social life.

1. Go through your notes and make a mark by every relevant comment, response, or observation. Some researchers prefer to do this type of review in the margins of hard-copy notes; others, on screen. Either way, don't be too discriminating at this stage; it is better to include too

> If you have the time and resources, the coding and sorting process can be done electronically, with a program such as *The Ethnograph* <http://www.qualisresearch.com/> or *NVivo* <http://www.qsrinternational.com/products_nvivo.aspx>.

much than too little. Use a relevant word or "code" in the margin to highlight what is important about that section of data.

2. Extract the relevant pieces of data you marked in step 1 so that they can be grouped and categorized. You can do this by hand copying or photocopying and cutting and pasting the relevant excerpts from your notes onto note cards, or by electronically blocking and copying the identified sections into a separate file. Whatever approach you take you should be able to see the bits of data side by side, just as you would for information in a library research paper (see Chapter 7). It may seem old-fashioned to use actual cards, but many students and faculty members still consider them the most effective device for organizing their notes.

3. Now consider what the information on each card or segment tells you about the setting you observed and/or the people you interviewed. Look for patterns among your data excerpts. Move them around to illustrate to yourself how the information fits together. For example, you might combine cards or blocks of data to which you assigned the same code in step 1 because they contain examples of the same kind of behavior, or you might arrange data sections to reflect stages in a process.

   Course materials and the assignment may also help identify patterns in your data. Recall concepts covered in the class that are relevant to your project. Gloria Fong, the student author of the sample ethnographic paper that appears at the end of this chapter, was asked by her instructor to observe and write about an aspect of college student life. Several class readings, including the classic work by Horowitz (1987) that she cites, focused on how college students do and don't feel engaged in their studies. In organizing her data, she might have listed the different roles that Horowitz noticed students take, then stacked in separate piles or moved to separate electronic files the data excerpts that illustrated them. Or she could have arranged her description of students in the "back of the class" in stages: as they selected their seats; began their nonacademic activities; and moved from one activity to another.

Some common themes ethnographers look for include the ways members characterize their group; the ways they distinguish between insiders and outsiders; the special language they develop to describe their shared activities and values; the ways they teach new members the ropes; the ways they identify and respond to objectionable behavior; the ways in which members experience their setting through the course of an event, a workday, or any other unit of experience; and their patterns of interaction. You may find some or all of these reflected in your notes, and you may find interesting themes not listed here. Depending on what your assignment is, you may choose to focus on one area or on several related themes.

WRITING YOUR PAPER

Unless your instructor suggests otherwise, the three-part essay format discussed in Chapter 2, with a few modifications, is typically the most appropriate format for this type of paper. Instead of organizing your paper around three or more "claims" or "points" that support a thesis, organize your paper around three or more themes identified in your field notes or three or more points that support one theme. Remember that you are responsible for demonstrating, through effective use of your data, a convincing description and analysis of your setting. Be sure to describe your research methods—where you went, how long you stayed, with whom you spoke, etc., and include illustrative excerpts from your field notes as evidence.

Several writing approaches are acceptable to report on your observations. One approach is to describe what happened or what was said, chronologically, and comment on how course concepts apply. Another approach is to organize your paper around concepts, defining and indicating the importance of each, and using your data as illustrations. You can follow the three-part essay format and use a selected concept or group of concepts for your main points. With any approach it is important to frequently return to course concepts and themes. Ask yourself how the events or comments you are describing reflect or illustrate sociological ideas. This will help you avoid the common mistakes of being too descriptive or making overly psychological interpretations of people you observe or interview. You can either work from your field notes and seek a concept from the course or take concepts from the course and seek examples in your field notes. This should lead to a deeper understanding of your field setting. For example, your field notes may indicate that a particular person was often labeled by others as "weird" or "dorky." Your course may have taught you that treating people as deviant is one way that groups enforce norms. Then you can ask what norms the group was enforcing when it singled out and picked on that individual.

Unless your instructor tells you otherwise, is important to incorporate your own reactions into your paper. Inevitably those engaged in ethnographic field research encounter people, events, and experiences that fascinate, surprise, confuse, or even upset them. It is a challenge to make effective use of these reactions without getting sidetracked into self-analysis. Question what your personal reactions reveal about the setting. Describe how your own feelings and thoughts helped you understand the people you studied and their interactions.

When writing your paper, quote your field notes directly and punctuate and cite them like any other source. Summarizing an incident or a response with an anecdote is an effective way to illustrate a theme. As long as they are relevant to your assignment, use your collected data in a variety of ways as they are the empirical basis for your discussion.

SUGGESTED READINGS

Denzin, Norman K. and Yvonna S. Lincoln. 2011. *The SAGE Handbook of Qualitative Research.* 4th ed. Thousand Oaks, CA: Sage Publications.

Emerson, Robert M., Rachel I. Fretz, and Linda L. Shaw. 2011. *Writing Ethnographic Fieldnotes.* 2nd ed. Chicago, IL: University of Chicago Press.

Merriam, Sharan B. 2002. *Qualitative Research in Practice: Examples for Discussion and Analysis.* San Francisco, CA: Jossey-Bass.

Warren, Carol A. B. and Tracy X. Karner. 2009. *Discovering Qualitative Methods: Field Research, Interviews, and Analysis.* 2nd ed. New York, NY: Oxford University Press.

A SAMPLE STUDENT PAPER

The following sample ethnographic field research paper was written by Gloria Fong for a class on the sociology of student and campus culture. She describes how she came to focus her research on the nonacademic activities of students in classroom settings. She observed students' activities both in a large lecture hall and in a small seminar room, noting where the students sat and their behavior during the lecture.

Gloria used her original data to answer three research questions. Her findings are illustrated by specific observations, which she summarized in her field notes. Sometimes her field notes and interview notes are quoted directly, and sometimes they are incorporated into the text of her paper.

Gloria's paper demonstrates that she is a capable and diligent student. Her creative brainstorming resulted in an attempt to fill a hole in the research literature on higher education. Although research has examined students' academic activities and their out-of-class activities, little is known about their nonacademic activities in classroom settings.

OUR COMMENTS

INTRODUCTION

Researchers in higher education have been interested in the ways that students either are or aren't involved in their college experience (Astin 1993; Horowitz 1987). There seems to be quite a lot of research about the academic activities of students in the classroom and about the nonacademic activities of students outside of the classroom. But there is not much about the nonacademic activities of students in academic settings. No one seems to have really researched in depth what students actually do in class, even though it is certainly a part of student and campus culture. Such data could certainly help improve the quality of the college experience, particularly by helping faculty understand how things look from the students' point of view.

RESEARCH DESIGN AND METHODS

I originally was interested in studying fashion on campus, but because there were already so many students in the class studying that, I was assigned to study something about academics. I spent a while trying to figure out what aspect of academics I wanted to look at most. Then in class the professor suggested that somebody look at where students sit in classrooms. Then another student in the class suggested that I look at how students do the daily crossword puzzle all the time during classes. As I was walking home after class, I started thinking back to all of the lectures and seminars I have been in during my four years in college, and realized that the back of the class is usually more interesting than the front of the room because of the nonacademic activities that take place. And so it came to me in a flash that I should just combine the two topics suggested to me in class and explore where people sit in classrooms and what people do

1

Gloria's first paragraph introduces her research question: In what nonacademic activities do students engage in a college classroom? Then she shows how it fits into existing research literature in higher education and indicates its significance.

Gloria's writing would be stronger if she used fewer adverbs. The words "really," "certainly," and "certainly" a second time add nothing. They are unnecessary attempts to make the text seem stronger, and would be unmissed if they were omitted.

Gloria's informal narrative style (telling about her walk home and how the question came to her "in a flash") was acceptable for this assignment, which was meant to lead to a preliminary research report. It might not be appropriate for more formal research papers.

depending on where they sit in class. The amount of time that it took me to string the suggested topics together to make my own topic shows how strongly people tend to separate the two realities of academics and nonacademics.

I became an ethnographer to investigate, (1) whether there is a front-of-the-room culture and a back-of-the-room culture, (2) whether students from one racial or economic background are more likely than others to sit in the front or the back of the classroom; (3) whether there is a difference between what students do in the back of the room in large lectures and what students do who sit in the back of the room in small seminars. I made various observations and inscriptions during one three-hour seminar I attended and one two-hour lecture I attended. I sat in the back of the classrooms and took notes on what students were doing and I also asked a few of the students I had observed some quick questions after each class was over. I recorded small notes to myself while in the classes I chose to attend. I then took the inscriptions I made in the classroom back home and turned them into formal field notes, which I later reviewed for themes and patterns (see Appendix A).

FINDINGS

In reviewing my field notes, I found answers to my three questions. First, there are definitely separate areas in the front and back of the lecture hall, which can be seen either from where people are sitting or from who is talking to whom. Second, social factors such as race, ethnicity, gender, and class standing did not seem to affect who sat in the back of a class versus who sat in the front of a class. Third, nonacademic activities take place in both overall settings (lecture hall or seminar room).

Even though it wasn't part of my original questions, I also learned something about why students bother going to class when they are doing so

Gloria included her interview notes and field notes as an appendix to her paper, which will allow her instructor and any other readers to review the detailed data she collected. (However, because of space limitations for this book, Appendix A is not included at the end of her paper here.)

In introducing this section, Gloria clearly identifies her major findings and organizes them around her research questions. This will serve as a road map for someone reading her findings.

Be careful to use the correct form of pronouns. Gloria has appropriately used "whom" as the object of the preposition "to."

It is not unusual that in the course of qualitative research, new insights lead to additional questions.

2

many other things besides listening to the lecture. This was a question that came to my mind while I was doing my research.

Is there a back of the room culture?

The "front" and "back" areas in the lecture hall were easy to see because they were physically separated.

> There are three main sections of seats, a left, right, and middle section. The right and left sections each consist of fourteen rows of seats with three seats across each row. The middle section consists of thirteen rows of seats with eight seats across each row. . . . The class is not full at all, and only the first five rows and the last two rows of the room have students in the seats.

> The middle of the room was basically a no-man's-land. When it comes to interactions, it seemed that only those who sat in the front of the class spoke with and/or interacted with the students in the front of the class. And furthermore, only those who sat in the back of the class spoke with and/or interacted with the students in the back. The nonacademic activities that I observed in the back of the class were: sleeping, eating, talking, doing the crossword puzzle from the school newspaper, doodling, and listening to music. And with the exception of listening to music, all of the nonacademic activities were low tech. I did not observe anyone text messaging on their cell phones, playing with portable video game devices, talking on their cell phones, or any other types of high-tech, nonacademic activities in the back of the room.

In the seminar room, there was no space for the "front" and "back" to be physically separated.

> In the middle of the room is a large rectangular table with sixteen chairs around it, seven on each long side of the table and two individual chairs at each end of the table. The room is cramped, to say

3

| Gloria quotes her field notes directly to illustrate the distribution of students in the classroom. |

| Gloria's notes do a good job of setting the scene for the reader. We can easily visualize the setting she was observing. |

| This is an effective contrast between the lecture hall and the seminar room. She might have made it more vivid with "In contrast to the lecture hall" at the beginning. |

the least. There are fifteen students and one professor. The students sit around the table, and the professor sits at the head of the table.

Before I observed the classes, I thought for sure that there would be less of a "back of the room" culture in a seminar room because of its size. I was surprised to find so many people doing the same types of nonacademic activities in both academic settings. The back of the room in the seminar was just as active with nonacademic activities as the back of the lecture hall. It is interesting to note that even though there were only 15 people in the seminar, there was still definitely a "back of the class" area. All the people sitting four seats or closer to the professor sat quietly and wrote down notes in their notebooks. They did not look at other people in the class and only looked up at the professor or the board when he was writing things down. All the people sitting five seats or more away from the professor felt that they were far enough away from him to be able to do other things besides take notes. This was the "back of the class" area for the seminar room.

Sociologists are always interested in the role of social factors in the type of experience under study. This conclusion was made possible by Gloria's detailed field notes, which included descriptions of social characteristics of the students she observed, and by her interviews, in which she asked students about their class standings (first year, sophomore, etc.).

Are students of certain social characteristics more likely to be in the back of the room?

There is no one type of person who sits in the back of the room and engages in nonacademic activities. All races, ethnicities, genders, and class standings are represented in the back of the room. Students' social characteristics did not appear to play a role in how involved they are in the academic part of what goes on in the classrooms.

Do nonacademic activities take place in both lecture halls and seminar rooms?

Before I observed the classes, I thought for sure that there would be less of a "back of the room" culture in a seminar room because of its size. I was surprised to find so many people doing the same types of nonacademic activities in both academic settings. The back of the room in the seminar was just as active with nonacademic activities as the back of the lecture hall.

Two females are each sitting seven seats away from the professor, directly across the table from each other, one on the left and one on the right side of the table. During the seminar meeting, these two females pass back and forth female A's copy of a newspaper clipping and female B's open notebook. I can see that the two students are doing the campus newspaper's daily crossword puzzle together, even though they are across the table from each other. They signal to each other when they need help, and take turns filling in blanks of the crossword puzzle. They both look up at the professor periodically to see where he is in the room so they do not get caught. Neither of them seems to notice that they are being very obvious with their passing the crossword puzzle and notebooks back and forth across the table.

But because the professor was very close to them, students in the seminar setting did check on where he was looking and what he was doing far more often than the people in large lecture halls checked.

Why do students engage in nonacademic activities while in class?

This wasn't one of my original research questions, but after observing students engaged in nonacademic activities during class, I became curious about why they bothered to attend class at all. Two of my interview subjects indicated that they wanted to be sure that they don't miss something that may be on a test. As one student put it:

> I try really hard to take notes but then I just space out. But I don't want to skip lecture because then I might miss something that is on the final.

This kind of unexpected finding is not unusual for qualitative research and makes it especially interesting.

5

There also seems to be a strong norm among students that one has to go to class to feel like, and appear as, a "good student." Being a "good student" means you attend all of your classes. One of the students I interviewed said, "I feel like I have to come to lecture, so I come."

DISCUSSION AND IMPLICATIONS

In my study, there were distinct groups in the front and in the back of the classroom. This is like the "OUTSIDERS" and the "COLLEGE MEN AND WOMEN" that Horowitz (1987) described in higher education. She describes college men and women as those students for whom "classes and books exist [only] as a price one has to pay for college life. . . . but no real college man or woman ever expects to live in the classroom" (1987:12). The outsiders are "studious, polite, and respectful of authority. . . . hardworking students [who] sought the approval of their teachers, not of their peers" (1987:14).

The findings are relevant to campus policy and programming because they could lead to some changes in campus policy and programming that are aimed at decreasing the amount of nonacademic activities in the back of classrooms directly. However, while there are obviously a lot of nonacademic activities occurring in lectures and seminars, I do not feel that there is really any reason to try and stop them, and really no way to stop them, because there is already an established culture of students sitting in the back of the room sleeping, eating, reading, etc. I feel that no matter what rules and regulations are put in place to stop them, there will always be students in the back of the class doing other things besides taking notes. This is because there will always be students who are just showing up to class to appear as a "good student," but not to take notes.

Instead, I would suggest that classes not be scheduled earlier than

Gloria effectively links her own observations with concepts from sociological studies. However, there is no need for capitalization here.

Gloria could have made her analysis even richer by pointing out an important difference between her observations and Horowitz's analysis, which suggests that "outsiders" and "college men and women" were of different racial and ethnic groups and different social classes.

6

11:00 A.M. to cut down on the amount of sleeping in class. Classes should also not be longer than two hours so students do not get bored and fidgety. Classes should not be scheduled around mealtimes so that people will not have to eat in class or fall asleep in class from being too tired from not eating. Also, I think online classes, video classes, or other types of distance learning should be considered for large lectures.

My findings could also be used to help foster a better understanding between students and faculty and therefore better relationships between the two, which would facilitate students' academic and personal development.

REFERENCES

Appropriately, Gloria started her References on a separate page.

Astin, Alexander. 1993. "Effects of Involvement." Pp. 365–395 in *What Matters in College? Four Critical Years Revisited,* edited by A. Astin. San Francisco, CA: Jossey-Bass.

Gloria should have included her interview and/or field notes in her list of references. Since the format was not specified in the assignment, she should have discussed the required information and preferred format with her instructor. Here is one possibility:

Fong, Gloria. May 11, 2004. Field notes, observations of seminar room, Los Angeles, California.

Horowitz, Helen Lefkowitz. 1987. "Introduction: The Worlds that Undergraduates Make." Pp. 3–22 in *Campus Life: Undergraduate Cultures from the End of the Eighteenth Century to the Present.* New York: Alfred A. Knopf.

Finishing Up

It has long been an axiom of mine that the little things are infinitely the most important.

SHERLOCK HOLMES IN SIR ARTHUR CONAN DOYLE'S
"A Case of Identity"

First impressions count. What your paper *looks* like is important; a professional-looking paper promises quality, so take the time to proofread and polish your paper before you submit it. Although a nicely presented paper that lacks substance will not likely fool even the weariest instructor, studies reveal that a professional-looking paper often contributes to a better grade.

EDITING

Edit your draft for spelling errors and punctuation, repeated words and phrases, and omitted words. Once you print what you hope will be your final draft, set the paper aside for several days, if possible. Efficiency in spotting weaknesses will increase and flaws will be more obvious after a brief break from editing.

Proofreading your paper will allow you to spot mechanical problems within your text. To proofread efficiently, you must *see*, not just *look at*, your draft. The way to *see* errors is to examine a *hard copy* of your paper by using a pen or pencil and pointing to each word as you read it to yourself. Many people's spoken grammar is better than their written grammar. Reading out loud

A computer tip.

By using your word processor's spell check you can locate and correct misspellings in your paper. However, do not depend solely on spell-check as it only identifies misspelled words if they do not appear in the English language at all, and it cannot identify improper word use, for example, "then" in place of "than." Additionally, while a word processor's spell check cannot detect redundant passages or incorrect sentence structure, most programs are able to check grammar and style. Although not foolproof, it can be a useful aid.

will help you detect problems with sentence structure and poor grammar that you might not notice reading silently. It may seem awkward at first, but it is a common technique also used by professors and professional writers. Once you have proofread your paper, have someone else proofread it, too.

FORMATTING

Begin by setting up the automatic formatting features on your computer. To ensure the paper's formatting remains consistent when you print, use the tab key, not the space bar, for indenting. Formatting guidelines include:

- Margins (one to one-and-a-half inches on all sides)
- Double-spacing (quotations longer than five lines should be single-spaced and indented one inch from the left margin)
- Paragraph indentions (one-half to one inch)
- Left margin justification. Do not justify the right margin; a ragged right margin is friendlier and the spacing between the letters looks better.
- A header with your last name and the page number only

This stage of preparing your paper is an opportunity to experiment with typeface, font, italics, boldface, boxes, borders, underlining, etc. However, to avoid adding too much page design and distracting the reader, keep these design principles in mind:

- What you do to the printed words should emphasize their meaning. For example, 12-point Helvetica Narrow is excellent for tables and other types of writing that require lots of information in a small space. Zapf Chancery is a display face that gives headings a decorative look; New Century Schoolbook looks traditionally academic.
- Use restraint. If you emphasize everything, nothing stands out.
- Use your page Preview function or scroll through the document to identify and repair "widows," which are single lines separated from the rest of their paragraph by a page break or other breaks, such as captions separated from figures.
- Use 12-point fonts; smaller ones are hard to read.
- Italicize titles of publications.
- Use boldface for emphasis, not italics, underlining, or capitalization.
- Simplicity is best.

If you use a title page, center your title horizontally halfway down the page. In the lower right-hand corner, put your name, course number, your instructor's name, and the date. Number pages beginning with the first page of the text, not with the title page. Some instructors do not require a title page for short papers (approximately five or fewer pages). If you're not using a title page, put your name, course number, and your instructor's name in the upper right-hand corner of page 1, triple-space and center the title, and triple-space again before you begin the first paragraph.

A review of Chapter 5 will remind you how to cite sources within the text of your paper as well as how to format the list of references that follows the text.

Depending on the type of paper you've written, some instructors may want you to include your raw data, statistical calculations, questionnaires, observation checklists, instructions to respondents, ethnographic field notes, or other items. These items can be added as an appendix to your paper. The Appendix follows the References or Bibliography on a separate, titled page. If your paper requires more than one appendix, number or letter them individually (i.e., Appendix 1, Appendix 2; or Appendix A, Appendix B, etc.) as if they were a continuous part of the text pages. You may single-space or double-space an appendix, depending on the nature of the material and how it can most easily be read; however, the heading is ordinarily centered and triple-spaced—you triple-space between "Appendix" and the title and triple-space again between the title and the body of the appendix.

As with any work created on a computer, save your document often and back it up or e-mail it to yourself as an attachment.

A CHECKLIST FOR SUBMITTING YOUR PAPER

1. Can you quickly identify your thesis or your hypothesis?
2. Does your thesis, or the logic behind your hypothesis, remain evident and central throughout the paper?
3. Do you support your thesis, or hypothesis, with adequate evidence? One trick for checking the quantity and quality of your evidence is to put a mark in the margin of a rough draft wherever you see evidence for your thesis, or hypothesis, pausing at each point to review its soundness. Instructors sometimes use this method when evaluating the reasonableness of an argument.
4. Is there a clear, logical relationship among all the sentences and paragraphs? If one is irrelevant to your thesis or hypothesis, delete it; if one veers off topic, rework it to ensure you stick to the subject.
5. Does the writing flow between generalizations and specifics that support and clarify those generalizations?
6. Are there smooth transitions between paragraphs? Sometimes transitions create themselves naturally during the writing process; other times you have to create them. The smoothest transitions come in the first sentence of each paragraph, referring back to where you came from and looking forward to where you are headed.
7. Do all your words mean what you think they mean? Be careful when using terms that have become part of everyday language yet retain special sociological definitions. If you're uncertain about the sociological definitions of your key terms, you might find them quickly in

"The difference between the almost right word and the right word is really a large matter—'tis the difference between the lightning-bug and the lightning."

Mark Twain

sociology textbooks by using the index and/or glossary, or in online dictionaries of sociological terms. A thesaurus is helpful in providing synonyms that can vary your word choice as well as locate a word that accurately expresses what you want to say. However, before you use a synonym double-check its meaning.

8. Have you looked carefully for errors in style (i.e., sentence structure, punctuation, spelling, citations)? As we mentioned in Chapter 3, reference books that present style guidelines are available online (see page 41) as well as in bookstores and libraries.

9. Have you eliminated all contractions? If you do not know your instructor's preference, avoid using contractions.

10. Have you stated your conclusion clearly and forcefully? A reader should have a clear understanding of what your main and minor points are.

11. Have you avoided sexist language?

12. Does the paper's formatting and reference system conform to your instructor's preferences? Have you used a consistent font, type size, and line spacing throughout the paper? Is page numbering turned on? Is the title page properly formatted? Are figures, graphs, or tables properly numbered?

13. Have you run your word processor's spell check?

THINKING BIG

If you or your instructor is particularly pleased with the quality of your paper, you might consider submitting it for presentation at a national or regional meeting of a professional sociological association or for publication in a scholarly journal. Paper presentations and publications that demonstrate good communication skills will increase your chance of getting into graduate school and will enhance your résumé.

The main professional organization in sociology is the American Sociological Association (ASA). The ASA holds an annual national meeting for the presentation of both theoretical and empirical research. Usually, several sessions are devoted to undergraduate and graduate student papers. The International Sociology Honor society, Alpha Kappa Delta (AKD), also holds both regional and national meetings at which students have the opportunity to present their work. Ask your instructor or undergraduate counselor for more information about these and other professional associations.

If you wish to submit your paper for publication in a scholarly journal, refer to the list in Chapter 4. You can find the name and address of the current editor and the guidelines for submission inside the most recent issue of the journal. Ask your instructor how to draft a cover letter to accompany your paper submission.

References

American Sociological Association. 2010. *American Sociological Association Style Guide.* 4th ed. Washington, DC: American Sociological Association.

Becker, Howard. 1986. *Writing for Social Scientists: How to Start and Finish Your Thesis, Book, or Article.* Chicago, IL: University of Chicago Press.

Conley, Dalton and Neil G. Bennett. 2000. "Is Biology Destiny? Birth Weight and Life Changes." *American Sociological Review* 65(3):458–67.

Durkheim, Emile. [1897] 1951. *Suicide.* Translated by J. A. Spaulding and G. Simpson. Glencoe, IL: Free Press.

Fischer, David Hackett. 1970. *Historians' Fallacies: Toward a Logic of Historical Thought.* New York: Harper & Row.

Gibaldi, Joseph. 1998. *MLA Style Manual and Guide to Scholarly Publishing.* 2nd ed. New York: Modern Language Association of America.

Goffman, Erving. 1959. *The Presentation of Self in Everyday Life.* Garden City, NY: Doubleday.

Hacker, Diana, and Nancy Sommers. *The Bedford Handbook.* 8th ed. Boston, MA: Bedford/St. Martin's.

Mills, C. Wright. [1959] 2000. *The Sociological Imagination.* New York: Oxford University Press.

Turabian, Kate L. 2007. *A Manual for Writers of Term Papers, Theses, and Dissertations.* 7th ed. Chicago, IL: University of Chicago Press.

The University of Chicago Press. 2003. *The Chicago Manual of Style.* 15th ed. Chicago, IL: University of Chicago Press.

Weber, Max. 2002. *The Protestant Ethic and the Spirit of Capitalism.* Translated by Stephen Kalberg. 3rd ed. Los Angeles, CA: Roxbury Publishing Co.

Index